C000141155

To the Mumma

Until we meet again pretty La(

For my sisters

Cheryl, Beccy and Donna. I see her in you all. This is our story thank you for being part of it.

For Paul Hicks

My Hero without a cape, my constant support and source of wisdom. I love you.

For dear Michaela

Thank you for choosing me to be your lobster, my sweet beautiful Dumfacehead

For the grandchildren

Her legacy lives in you all, the future is yours. Dance well Adam, Kennedy, William, Owen, George, Charlie, Zack, Millie, Izzybell and Finn.

Foreword

Our journey across our wonderful country had far too many stops to include in one place, from the peak district to the ridings of Yorkshire we travelled them all. When we ran away we decided on a few rules, the most important being that every county on the map would be googled and the top search result for each county would be the first place travelled, followed by as many landmarks, forts, castles and gardens we could cram in. Our travels took us to filming locations for the Batman films and in stark contrast the ever so British Carry on films as well as sites of terrible murders and tragedy that are all sadly part of our rich tapestry.

The world is a beautiful place, the UK is unique, it has its heroes and villains celebrated equally as only we British know how. As life moves on at such a fast pace with phones recording and documenting our everyday lives it leaves very little for future historians to do, taking time to look back and understand a life less documented is fascinating to me, with each step I learned something about history, human nature and myself.

It was important for me to write about the places that I had links to as well as ones that I had always ways wanted to see but could never make the time to do so. To my utmost surprise there was also some places that completely blindsided me giving me the odd epiphany or two. There were times through my grief that a smell or a view could set me off on reminiscent pathways ultimately teaching me a little more about myself, as we travelled from the old to the new my views changed almost as often as the scenery. Self-discovery is a frightening thing sometimes but if you are lucky enough to find someone to lend you the strength to enable you to carry on, hold on to them with both hands and celebrate them, look after them and make them smile every opportunity that you have because you never know when they will be gone.

Finally stopping to look at things and literally smelling the roses from time to time did me the power of good. Understanding why we do things and how things work has become a passion for me, One thing I understand now about myself is that I'm very much a different person to the one I was in my twenties, withstanding my demons definitely held me back and pushed me into dark waters at times and I'm sure those around me often knew I was out of my depth and in need of but unable to ask for help. You eventually come through the other side where you are no longer able to walk so proud or talk so loudly, I accept my vulnerability and embrace it.

Learning from history is important, understanding the links from our own past and understanding the past mistakes of society will I know make us gentler and kinder to both ourselves and each other. Holding our tongues when comments are not needed and considering the impact rather than the intent of our words can make all the difference to others and life far more pleasant.

Words are as powerful as a loaded gun, and they can be hurtful, spiteful at times but used wisely and with thought they can be wonderful. I have learnt to choose my words wisely, each one considered and placed with care. I am still new to this and I don't always get it right, I feel empowered now to acknowledge and apologise when I get things wrong. I have two ears and one mouth, and I use them (I hope) in that proportion. You can learn much from people and places. If I can anyone can. The greatest discovery you are ever likely to make is that you are you, and that is OK to continue as you are, your body is the greatest tool you will ever have so be kind to it, no one can have your mind or your thoughts and no one is entitled to either one, unless we choose to let them, I now know however to choose well.

To anyone I ever hurt, I'm sorry. To those that I haven't said it too often enough I love you all.

Chapter One: Lost

Mum died, my world ended, and my life fell apart. The stark realisation that every family photograph taken from this moment on, would forever have the most important person missing dawned on me. I didn't like it, I was angry, my outlook changed. My perspective was gone and to coin an old show tune, and to remain true my usual clichéd self, CY Coleman I seem to recall wrote "the colours of my life are incomprehensible brown, the colour of the earth; in Gold I find no worth".

Nothing to me mattered now. My family, the ones that were left that is, lived over one hundred miles away on the Isle of Wight where I was now stood at the entrance to St Helen's hospital. The realisation that mum wasn't coming home with me whirled around my head like some poxy siren, it pierced through my head and shattered my thoughts; it felt like a tough and cruel test.

As I walked through the automatic hospital doors for the last time (I have never been back and never will this I swear) two rainbows appeared and as they taunted me from high up in the Newport sky I had no idea just how tough things would be and I had less of an idea of how far and wide the burden of loss would carry me, I didn't know then it would take me to every place in the United Kingdom that I had ever wanted to see, places of legend and adventure, places steeped in history throughout every period in great British history, from Bram stoker to Alfred the great, it took me to the edge of my own sanity and beyond far into the depths of despair, so deep in fact I never thought them possible. I doubted even that a place so deep and dark filled with such terror and rage, such blinding hate could have a point of return, it does, I did, but I'll come to that later. For now, I was an orphan and I was alone, completely, totally, it felt so final and true. I lacked only the ragged trousers.

It was September but it felt warm, yet I had no coat with me. This was my mum's last act of love, an escort to the car free from the rain and misery of the season, the violent Solent air stream was whipping up gusts of cold mocking wind and rain, the sea I'm told could always be cruel, I opened the car door and shut the world out, as the door clunked behind me, I sat thinking, my brain so scrambled that I had to remember how the bloody car started, all combinations of pedals, buttons and levers flowed through my mind as the car serenaded my mum up to heaven with a chorus of that old favourite "please fasten your seatbelt".

I had no coat with me as I had been working in Harold Hill, Essex one hundred and thirty miles and a ferry ride away only a few hours earlier, it was a clear and fresh September morning there, almost warm as the summer had not quite ended there yet. I was supposed to have flown out to Newcastle the previous evening but something inside, a little voice maybe? had told me to cancel this business trip and stay local, something had bothered me the night before and I was compelled not to go, as I pondered this my phone rang, so as I sat in the car park of the Farnham Road Shopping Quadrant in Harold Hill the call, the one I had been dreading was happening.

It was my mum's partner on the other end of the line. All I remember about the content of this call is "mum, get here and quick" I fastened my seatbelt, at this point any memory of this particular journey still eludes me, one day I think perhaps on an idle Wednesday morning sat at my desk my brain will unlock this mystery and fill in the gap between my departure on from the mighty Quadrant(I do love a grand name, nothing says twat better than an episode of delusions of grandeur during a planning committee meeting in some arsehole conference room) to my arrival at the exit door of the Newport hospital and I'm more that certain that this car ride is a whole other story, hopefully sans explosions and daring stunts of the General Lee variety. Weeks passed.

I returned from the terrible funeral on a terrible ferry nursing a terrible coffee in a terrible mood. In the interests of full disclosure I must admit here to you all and to the Solent Port Authority and all their agents that I did eventually toss the terrible coffee into the terrible dark waters, I also admit for the second time in these short lines that I paraphrased again another far better wit than I,(being short of any original thoughts of my own) Tony Hancock, of the tortured genius English comedy variety that as I tossed the coffee overboard I shouted to no one other than a startled seagull and a surprised retired greyhound called Mervin "oh what's the bloody point!" you see everything within me was gone, not just the terrible coffee.

The funeral was horrible. I decided against staying on the Island. There was a family drink scheduled a few hours after the funeral tea, I often wondered how perverse the English language is you have a wedding breakfast and a funeral tea, but this is something that I must not digress about now. I could however see no point in sitting in a pub censoring my thoughts and listening to stories about the good old days while I quietly selected those present that I wished were dead instead of my beautiful mum.

This I understood later from a nice but ineffectual quinoa eating therapist called Hugo that this was part of the grieving process. I met with Hugo in a professional capacity only once which was enough for me to ascertain that he was probably, responsible for the god-awful situation the country now finds itself in where everyone is in fear of everything and we are all expected to cry and man up, be happy yet sad all at the same time while simultaneously remaining cognitive of all social and gender equality issues (No wonder the fucking pandas refuse to breed) I am entirely convinced though that he was a full card carrying twat of the highest order of twats and would if ever he was re incarnated as an animal, as he assured me he would be I'm certain he would be eaten by another perhaps slightly more switched on and far less twatty animal perhaps an aardvark) This realisation cost AXA insurance £60 and me an hour of my life that thus far I have not been able to get back.

Back to my point, I had left mum for the last time at the crematorium, and yes you are right, the crematorium was terrible. My family were reeling still from the day. I remember the service now; it took me five years for my brain to open this memory and allow me to play it. It's something that I do less and less often these days. I find now my memories are of happier times, I can hear mum's voice and I can remember her wisdom, memories formed from echoed laughter if you will. But for the now, the reality of the funeral, the smell of the hall, the murmuring of the people was too much.

There is no such thing as a good funeral or a nice funeral, they are all awful and they are never made better regardless of how much you spend or how you dress them up. They mark a loss, a space, they drive home the dreadful conclusion that a person who is loved, who will always be loved, and could never be replaced is gone, and they aren't coming back. This realisation is when I'm certain my heart actually broke.

On a whim, I packed my things quietly, this act of defiance was carried out quietly as I was later told that no one heard me pack, I opened the front door to my mum's house and got in my car, pointed it towards Fishbourne ferry terminal and headed home towards Kent. It was in Kent where I was sure I would end my life and free myself of the misery within.

This may seem very ordinary now, and I may be getting ahead of myself but something strange happened to me when the doors of the Wightlink Ferry were hauled open grunting under the strain of their own weight and the front wheels of my Audi touched down on the mainland, I had successfully resisted the urge to throw myself in the murky water. Resisting suicide (sounds like a terrible rock album title) made me hungry and I now had an overwhelming feeling of hunger. It bore into me and my head started to swim, at this point I realized that my thoughts of suicide were only fleeting. My stomach had won out over my heart and had also successfully overruled my head. My stomach the victor, had engaged in a defiant act of self-preservation. Food not bloodshed prevailed, but again I'm going ahead of myself.

The act of killing oneself is quite a consideration, how dramatic should it be, who will find me and what will I wear! The organisation that was required was just too much for my poor bereaved brain to be bothered with. In any sense, the love I have for my two sons far outweighed any real notion of a serious attempt and anyhow I really couldn't think outside the box enough to make my departure truly epic and as my mum had said if something is worth doing it is worth doing well. I merely flirted with the idea of death, a casual thought, a pause on my life, a footnote to this rather macabre revelation is I never thought of suicide again it is now just a memory committed here to the page for everyone to see. It's not something I talk about and perhaps not something many people know that I considered but if not for a second on that fateful night I may not have been here now writing these words and sharing my story. Suicide is the result of a malfunctioning mind, it is the loneliest feeling in the world, it is as close to "feeling" death for one's self that I think humankind can experience.

My stomach was victor and as the majority shareholder it had steered me victorious to a small chip shop, for those of you who love fish and chips the one in question is Cockhill's on Queens Street in Portsmouth. It is truly awesome.

Fresh from the ferry and lamenting upon my act of vandalism and fearing that the ramifications of the Solent Port Authority for littering would be devastating and wide-reaching (the signs told me so) and given that I was now ravenously hungry, I decided to get off the street and hide in the chip shop, there is something about a funeral spread whether it's lavish or humble it's just not enjoyable. I wanted no part of my mum's funeral tea, I didn't to be honest want the funeral, and I didn't want the music, the black cars or any of the small talk.

I just wanted it to be done so that I could concentrate on my Follie into the afterlife, a most grand adventure if you will. That's how it was in my mind and I was making apologies for it and even as I reflected on my exit from this realm I realised that despite my best efforts to be a suicide statistic I was in fact Winnie the bloody Pooh (a most grand adventure?) Christ could that be any more perverse? And in any case any suicide bid that involves Winnie the Pooh is just too tragic to contemplate almost like witnessing Noddy facing a firing squad.

 It's not the fish and chips that are strange about the story more though what happened when I walked into the little shop, I had been here many times before; the smell was a welcome relief from my troubles. A kindly man appeared from the back and told me how lucky I was as he was about to close, I instantly asserted my right to be British and apologised and offered to leave then being even more British I contemplated telling him to fuck off and that my mum was dead (we all think like that sometimes don't we?) The gentleman was called Kevin he told me he didn't have anywhere to be going and would be pleased to fry me anything if I didn't mind the wait and I was suitably relieved that I hadn't indeed told him to fuck off. This simple act of kindness was music to my ears. I ordered my Mum's favourite cod and chips and waited at the counter as Kevin dropped the cod into the fryer and proceeded to secure his shop for the night and dutifully continue his closing routine.

It was here that I presented another altogether different and most welcomed stage of bereavement, denial and I should say this so far was my favourite stage, denial allowed me to be anyone. As I toyed with the idea of re-inventing myself as Maurice a space cowboy, I chose rather unconvincingly to be me, but this version of me, the one who had been so British moments earlier had a mum, she was on the Isle of Wight, very much alive sat in her favourite chair where I had left her merely hours before watching television and talking on the phone to my sisters telling them what a great weekend we had had and then went on to start planning her birthday and the oncoming Christmas season. Mum loved Christmas and made it special always.

As I chatted to Kevin I told him about the things my mum and I had been doing together, we had visited Blackgang Chine, the needles and I told him of how we had walked around the shops of Newport complaining they aren't as good as the ones in Lakeside In Essex or at Bexleyheath in Kent and as usual we hadn't found anything to buy, but that was all right because when mum came to visit me next month we would go to her favourite shops and we would find plenty of ideas for her birthday and for Christmas gifts. Before I knew it, I had recounted happy memories of holidays spent with my family on the Isle of Wight over many years. The walks to the sand park in Ryde, the pier in Sandown and all the time we spent at Robin Hill Country Park with all her grandchildren It gets a bit dark here, but don't worry I'll hold your hand and lead you back to the light very soon!

Painfully it was at Robin Hill where the last photo of my whole family was taken with my mum one year and one month before her death. This picture sits on my shelf at home, one day I hope to turn it upwards so that I can see it, but for now it is turned away, hanging in shame as the clues were all there but I was just too stubborn to see them, I know it is there and I'm happy because know where it is and where it will always be but for now it faces down. I face it down because the day the picture was taken was the day after my mum was told she had terminal cancer, she is there beautiful and smiling along with us all in the sunshine and in the company of her family, this incredible act of bravery, two fingers up at cancer, a woman knowing she is going to die and that she will have to say goodbye to all these smiling faces, loved ones that she held in her arms as babies and loved unconditionally. Pictured smiling with her whole family, her whole world knowing that this would be the last time that she wouldn't be missing from the picture (but never our hearts). Knowing that she won't see her beautiful grandchildren grow up and that her time was short. If this picture were a book it is one that you just wouldn't be able to read because the ending is just too tough to take.

My fish and chips were soon ready and as Kevin opened the now bolted door I thanked him for his time and kindness, as the cold and damp October air hit me as the door of the shop clicked shut, I walked a few paces to my car with the sense of loss washing over me. As I opened my car door I looked back at the little fish and chip shop eager for one more whimsical bout of storytelling with Kevin, this time I could recount the Christmas my aunt Viv got upset and had to be calmed with large amounts of brandy by my still sniggering mum but the interior was already dark and the place was now abandoned. The streetlights cast a powdering of light on the glass, enough so that a reflection appeared in front of me a shadow of a man in the window looking back; he was familiar but not friendly. He stood there with a chip bag in his hand and great fat tears running down his cheeks he looked beaten and I'm pretty sure then that he was. There stood only distance between him and home, it would be a long journey. One filled by silence, pain, chips, and regret.

I eased myself into my seat; it felt warm against the night. I placed the key into the ignition and the car sprung to life, the engine hummed and the dashboard lit up, the little LCD screen raised from its cocoon in the dashboard and Rod Stewart's kiss her for me played through the speakers. Misery overwhelmed me, I checked the rear-view mirror, engaged the gears, and headed for the motorway and home leaving the sad wanker in the shop window behind me, after all I was already AWOL from mum's funeral so the point of no return had already been passed and for the first time in a long time I didn't give one flying fuck, two big shits or any combination of the two. I felt liberated. My acts of defiance had awakened something, I didn't know this then but this night, this moment in a soggy corner of southern England was a turning point for me I was doing what pleased me for the first time ever, I didn't give a shit what the consequences were, it was here it was settled, If the good lord or whoever is in charge was going to take my mum aged only Fifty-Eight then the message to me was clear, we only dance on this earth a short while, message received and understood. I knew then that my life was about to change. I could be anyone and do anything I wanted if I put my mind to it.

As I haven't treated myself or you my dear readers to a cliché in a while I think it is apt to coin a few here to summarise my thinking on that cold night all those years ago, this will I hope give you a flavour as to my transformation as my car crossed the border of Hampshire into Kent, "the worm has turned", "tomorrow is another day", "what doesn't kill me makes me stronger" (said by someone who has never battled polio I imagine) and my favourite "fuck this for a game of soldiers".

I arrived home in Kent around 10pm that evening, the car's lights guided me onto my driveway, and the battered old blue garage door reflected my mood. The engine drew silent and the car fell dark. I sat feeling the darkness surround me, it was decided. I opened the car door; my journey was about to begin, and I was going to get the girl. I placed my foot on the wet driveway and took my first step towards the rest of my life.

Chapter Two: The daydream believer and the homecoming queen

I must state here, I have never been good with women. If I was to be featured on the front page of the national geographic or have my endeavours with the fairer sex narrated by Sir David Attenborough on the good old BBC, my efforts would be likened to an Albatross. I can hear Sir David now in his cathartic manner and a sympathetic voice charting my failure "the dance is sinful" he would lament as the other British birds up and migrated south for winter or any other place that I wasn't Sir David would continue "lonely Gary, like lonely George the tortoise continues gliding and crashing from one mixed up crazy mating ritual to another" he would observe that It's a wonder that I had managed to breed at all.

I have considered my failings often and I stumbled to the conclusion that my failings are self- inflicted and three-fold, the first issue is I have a modification microchip inserted firmly in my arse that doesn't allow me to ask any female out that I like, secondly, I have a second chip inserted (which I am yet to locate) that turns me into a complete moron when I see a pretty lady and that thirdly and perhaps more importantly is that I am male so I am pathologically programmed to be stupid when it comes to both feelings and the emotional needs of a mate. This really to be honest has me fucked, but not fucked in the pleasant way how most of us would like to be fucked, I am just fucked in the Anglo-Saxon sense that I'm up the creek without a paddle, I'm on the roof and I've lost my ladder and my car has shit in engine, a useful tip for anyone reading never when told by a mechanic that "you got shit in the engine" ask how often you have to do it! It just aggravates them, and they will Anglo-Saxon fuck you on the parts. Lesson learned; I move on.

So, when I said I was going to get the girl, what I really meant was that I was going to brood over her and not tell her how I feel, be all male and then watch her get taken by someone else and walk off into the sunset with him, get married, have children, and live happily ever after, so I decided that I would need to devise a plan that would not only be fool proof but brilliantly executed.

Herein lay my first two problems excluding the fact that I wasn't organised enough to kill myself just days earlier I was probably less than capable to devise a fool proof and brilliantly executed plan. It became plain to me that rather than being a James Bond type of guy I was more of the shamble along then fall over farting loudly as my trousers fall down as I did so kind of guy, fear not though as in any eventuality when one's trousers do fall down post fart I am familiar and skilled enough in this situation to merely step out of them and continue on unmentioned as a lady who has just lost her knickers might, but dear reader I have digressed once again, I will try to limit these follies as much as I can, back to my point; I was only missing two steps in my two-step plan.

It's not that I lack charisma you understand, I remember I was once accused of lacking charisma by an old perverted sex pest called Keith in the basement of Gamley's Toy store Bromley in 1992, Keith was what in the days before Human Resources and People teams would describe as a character.

He used to comb his remaining hairs over his balding head, you know it "the comb over style" this would be beautifully enhanced with a hair dye product so subtle that you could never tell he dyed his hair, he would exclaim to anyone who forgot or didn't know to ignore him "fifty eight and jet black hair" this "look" was topped off with a spray for balding gentleman of a certain age that would cover the bald spot with spray on hair, this miracle spray was as effective as giving yourself a going over with a can car paint. Stunning job Sir!

One day we were unloading a pre-Christmas delivery of Power Rangers and other sundry plastic Japanese consumer durables, this one December day it was so windy that his hair which was so diligently sprayed with hair lacquer that it began to lift like metal tea pot lid (you know the type) up and down it went in the wind, when he started whistling one of the delivery drivers shouted "Keith the kettle has boiled time to pour mate" Keith never got the joke that I was laughing hysterically along to, in his anger this is when Keith shouted angrily that we weren't funny and we all lacked said charisma, to which I replied "no I do not lack it" in a deadpan delivery that made us all laugh even more, see a response of absolute genius and a clear demonstration of my repartee! In hindsight, a simple fuck off Keith probably would have sufficed.

So, the plan that I didn't have and all the issues I have now explained stood in my way, the old me you must understand would at this point give up and bury his head in some computer game and throw himself into his work until the feeling had passed. The problem for me now, aside from the two microchips, being male and missing the two steps in my two-step plan was that my work no longer did it for me, losing mum had shifted my priorities (rightly so many of my friends would argue) but I'll come to that in a while.

I decided to head to the Bluewater Shopping centre to find myself a game to bury my head in, I was still off work at this point and my social life was extinct. After much searching it was evident that any good releases where lacking The shop didn't have a handy "for the recently bereaved" or "love sick" section full of games that hit spot, mum had died you see rather selfishly during a very dry period in the gaming calendar, I would have to wait for the Christmas titles to be released to a baying public before anything remotely suitable would be available to me, this is something that I intend to address with mum later, I'll let you all know how I get on.

So as I wondered about the shop with its promises of the lowest price guaranteed and apologies for having prices so low they had no stock I decided against asking for help, I'm not saying that the guy "Neil" in the store was odd but in 2006 a mile from the shopping centre there was an alarming case of donkeys going missing never to be seen again and I think without doubt Neil knows where they went and what happened to them, so thinking that approaching Neil and asking him what games would be suitable for the love sick or bereaved was not a good idea, I wondered what other awkward questions have been asked by other customers before "excuse me I'm a virgin what is a good game for a virgin please?" or "is this game suitable for someone who excessively masturbates?" or "I have low mood and self-esteem will this do for me?".

 A few years later I was discussing this very point with my sister Donna hit the nail on the head with her summation "Gary, those questions apply to ninety five percent of the computer game buying public, I don't think there is one copy of call of duty that isn't spattered with semen and covered in shame". Those games must have seen some things I thought. I left the shop without a game and with the more pressing issue at hand, this feeling I had wasn't going to go away.

I thought about the girl (I'll introduce you later) often. When mum was unwell, and I was sitting beside her bed at the hospital watching her sleep thoughts of the girl came to me at first only fleetingly but often. As mum slept more and I had more time to reflect, my thoughts turned to her almost always, she presented a route of escape from the four walls of the beige hospital interior. My thoughts led me to our first meeting and subsequent encounters that led me to my dilemma.

My first meeting with her got off to a disastrous start, at first sight she loathed me, she later described me as "all that and a greasy bag of chips" (it's an East London thing) she asked me to move out of her way in the small office, punched some things into a computer and left without a goodbye. In fact, I didn't even find out her name.

First impression ruined and microchips set to overload I bombed. In one glance and a few sentences she destroyed me; this is a quality she still has today. Luckily for me it is normally some bureaucrat or unhelpful over officious crackpot that gets destroyed while I hide shaking with laughter at her quick wit and no-nonsense approach. I had my work cut out and I had the feeling if I got this wrong, I may well have other things cut out or worse cut off!

Over the coming months and years in the lead up to mum's illness I had cause to see her more often as our paths crossed, this led eventually to me asking my good work friend Barry who this uptight rather prickly woman was, Michaela he said adding that she wasn't too bad really, she was just rather shy and could come across as a bit frosty, "A bit frosty" I remarked, "she is more like a nuclear winter!"

Time went on and things changed we chatted to pass the time on long working days as we applied ourselves to our various labours, although our conversation was casual it filled the awkward silences, before not too long it dawned on me that the awkward silences has evaporated and I was now starting to look forward to our conversations. I learned she liked American cars, Horror movies, gore a swell as reading and horse riding, the one thing that stuck out for me was how very well educated she is, far more so than me. She was clever both bookish and in real life, as time went on she let more of her personality through, small chinks to start with but in time she became comfortable with me, I found her also to be funny, observant and in some ways guarded, I felt she was completely unobtainable and out of reach for a man like me. I was the quintessential daydream believer and she was a real life home coming queen. Stunningly beautiful and perfect in every way. I learned in time that she had had a difficult upbringing and an unhappy home life growing up (that is her story to tell when she is ready) but I found we as adults were both sad in our own ways Michaela never said outright but it was an unspoken understanding, we were each surrounded by people but lonely, a very difficult situation to be in for anyone. In those days, I could be in a crowded room wanting to shout for the world to be stopped so that I could get off.

In Michaela, I found another lost soul, someone craving companionship and love, a fellow traveller looking for something not yet understood. I knew I loved her quite early on, but she was a clear ten and I well let us just say I was not. What could this well-educated, beautiful, and funny lady see in me? Her friendship meant more to me that a clumsy attempt to ask her out anyway I knew that she was taken, and it wasn't for me to break her relationship up. She was clearly off limits. I was just pleased to have her as a friend. A pause in my own chaotic little world. Perfect.

I was now enjoying my chats with Michaela at work and I had lost my nerve when it came to telling her how I felt I just didn't think it was appropriate, I didn't know how she would react, I had a fair idea how her partner of ten years would and I felt that I loved her enough to leave her alone and let her go. My work except Michaela now had no meaning and by this time my eyes were set firmly on the horizon.

Losing mum was like a shot from a cannon the initial blast was devastating but the reverberation was all encompassing and it consumed me. I couldn't sleep Edgar Allen Poe was right, sleep was like little slices of death to me, I was neither awake nor asleep I was just walking through time.

I couldn't eat and I was drowning in a sea of pity. In danger of losing my reason and I knew that I had to take control, I had to change. The surge of energy inside me was overwhelming. As I sat working at my desk in Enfield North London my mind wandered and

I was transported back to my childhood, I recalled stories of Arthurian Legends, Robin Hood, and heroic tales of the second world war when good could overcome evil these visions all extended out to the front of my mind.

I became excited of thoughts of seeing the sound mirrors and the coastal defences that beat Napoleon and Hitler, the richness of this great nation I lived in was beckoning me and I wanted to see it all, from carry on films to the industrial revolution I wanted to see it all for myself. I would walk back in history; I would learn I would keep going until there was nothing left to see, or my demons were driven from me.

I had to get away; there was no question in my mind. This time there would be no awkward situations or fumbled attempts of romance, no nonsense, no microchip, and no David Attenborough. Just me, my car, and the open road. I would miss Michaela for the rest of my life, of this I was sure. My mum however had other plans.

I resigned my position with One month's notice. It was decided. I needed some perspective and the only way it would come was to strike out and that at thirty-six years old I was going to do something that I had never done before, I was going to run away from home.

Chapter three: neither here nor there

It was my last day at work, a month had flown by, my only sadness was to be leaving My beautiful Michaela behind, not being able to see her and talk to her everyday was too much for me to bare, but bare I must I kept telling myself, it's for the best I was by now at best a walking cliché. I was still counting the time since my mum had died in days, I was a walking shell, nothing could lift me from the void I was feeling, I had started to avoid places that my mum and I had once known, the various coffee shops and high streets that had been so familiar and welcoming were now shadowy places filled with memories that I no longer wanted.

Irrational fear consumed me, I became frightened by things that weren't there, the life force was draining from me and I felt a persistently on edge. Never more so than one afternoon I was by myself walking down Orpington High street where I lived with my mum when I was a small boy, it was familiar to me like a comfortable old she, but today this comfortable old loafer felt odd, like a shoe with a penny stuck inside when you put it on, no big deal after all you can remove a penny from your shoe and move on, I was suddenly overcome with an illogical panic that I may see someone that used to know mum and they might ask me how she was, this on reflection struck me as odd as it had been more than 25 years since we had lived here and the chances of any such meeting was unlikely but non the less my heart raced at the prospect, denial shot through me as I felt my legs buckle, sickness engulfed me and as I stood there on the high street I was little boy again. I wanted to cry, I wanted to find a grown up that could help me, but stood there I was alone, completely.

Route master buses had not long been removed from the route between Sidcup and Green Street Green, great new buses had been added to the route with automatic doors encompassed within a box like design; this was the future the old guard was moving over for these new shiny forgettable pieces of progress. I remember how sophisticated I felt sat on this shiny new bus gleaming with a hopeful enthusiasm, I remember the smell as it wafted through me, I smelt the new plastic trim and the newly upholstered seats and even now almost thirty-five years on the smell of a new bus never fails to transport me back to those glorious days.

 I remember the new bus was sans a bloody great hole in the back, I remember I always had a feeling that I was sure to fall out of what to my seven-year-old mind seemed to be a fucking great gaping chasm and grind my face to mince during the process. A bloody good job too I thought.

On this particular day, my mum had lifted me off the bus to the pavement when the doors suddenly closed with a menacing hiss and the bus along with my mum was conveyed away in a cloud of diesel fumes. Stood there on the curb side frozen rigid with fear at the prospect of being whisked away by all manner of childhood monsters (monsters in the early eighties were far more imaginative back then parents really worked hard to scare the shit out of us, for instance there was the man who sat in the road and took his shoes and socks off- yes really, Trig Trog the troll who lived in the back alley behind my house and worst of all the poor innocent hard working bugger who drove the corona drink lorry that was according to all the local mums a grade A child poisoner- the poor bastard our mums would say anything to get out of buying a drink from him! but I will elaborate on him and the others later). The feeling of abandonment and panic I felt then was the same feeling I felt as I stood on pavement as a man, I wanted the bus to stop, I wanted my mum back, and I didn't want to be alone anymore. The terrible part of being a grownup was knowing that now the bus wasn't going to bring her back, nothing was. I died a little more that day. Sorrow is the loneliest friend and adulthood that once seemed so far away was here now staring me in the face goading me, making it worse.

I already knew that getting away was the right thing for me. I would never run into an old acquaintance or be in a familiar setting where my memories could terrify me. I was leaving everything behind and I was starting fresh. I wasn't sure where I was heading but my bags were packed, and I was leaving on Monday. My final working week passed as quickly as the preceding three weeks had dragged and Friday was over before I knew it, I was busy finishing my last handover in Hornchurch, an upscale hamlet in Essex just outside of Romford. I'm told that Hornchurch is such a treasure that several ex TOWIE "stars" have set up shops, (the TOWIE set call them boutiques, and the difference was explained to me. It seemed very simple in a boutique you pay double the price) these brilliantly conceived cavalcades were locally famous for selling all sorts of crazy, in one such "boutique" everything you desire for your poor enslaved Chihuahua can be purchased from a cup cake to a Dutch cap. (No wonder the poor bastards always looked surprised).

I was at last done; my agenda was clear. I gathered my things together in my battered old work bag while lamenting that my equally battered Franklin organiser would be better suited to enter a river at some point in the near future, I made a mental note to throw it during my travels I had the perfect place in mind (and in no time it would be drowned in shit) and as I stirred from my reverie I picked my bag up feeling its unnecessary heaviness as the straps pressed into my palms, as if it was burdened with my thoughts, although it would be much easier to get rid of my thoughts by throwing myself in the river than the bag.

I was getting ready to leave for the last time and to begin the next chapter of my life when Michaela appeared in the doorway of the office, she took my breath away she was wearing a white loose-fitting top with a tight sports type T shirt underneath, she had a black skirt flowing down to her ankles, her hair was newly styled and her make-up immaculate, It was then I realised this was the first time I had seen her in her civilian clothes with make-up on, she went from a clear ten to a hundred, she looked stunning and I looked like a rather sweaty turd holding a handbag.

I hadn't anticipated a goodbye with her, a sadness swept over me and I admit that the very hint of goodbye left me drained but there she was perfect, her eyes met mine and she smiled, my anally fixed microchip melted on sight instantly sending me spinning I knew that whatever happened next I was invariably going to be stupid, say something stupid or do both (what the hell, I had time) furthermore to set me off I now had images of myself farting and my trousers falling down as I met her gaze, achieving Hugo's dream of being both funny and sad simultaneously. I desperately thought to myself keep breathing, don't fart and step out of the trousers if they fall to my ankles if needed (this is now my life's mantra).

She had me, I was in her grip and I couldn't run this I knew was true as she was blocking my exit and there is never a window when you need it! as several more microchips exploded in my arse earth shattering warning sirens sounded in my head and I was staggering dangerously into wanker territory right in front of her, this is goodbye I thought, Do I shake her hand, Oh god don't fart, do I offer her a peck on the cheek, are my flies undone, don't fart do I give her a hug? all communication channels available to a normal human were no longer available to me and I was failing I had nothing but my own poor words to offer her, then out of nowhere the self-preservation society theme tune; the one from the Italian job started playing in my head, "get your skates on mate" I blurted out! (wanker wanker wanker) Michaela looked at me surprised "what?" she enquired, "I'd better get my skates on" I had brilliantly recovered. "Oh" she said, "I thought you were singing the Italian job theme, I love that film" Bollocks I thought.

It was here that Michaela threw me my first lifeline "we are all going out for a drink tomorrow evening if you want to come" the woman of my dreams said as shifted uneasily. Most normal people would at this point jump at the chance and proceed to write the impending details in blood, the rules for normal people when you are asked out by someone that you really fancy are as follows; if they offer you a dead human foot to eat, you eat it. If they invite you to watch contemporary interpretive dance dealing with issues arising from the outcry of the soul of their grandmother you go and you applaud with gusto at the end and lastly if they invite you for an evening out under no circumstances should you hesitate.

We all know now I am not good when it comes to love or matters of the heart and it's here that I must detail the first of my many malfunctions that day, when Michaela asked me in earnest to that simple works gathering, I took this simple concise piece of information and directed it straight to the microchip inserted firmly where the sun doesn't shine and I proceeded to cover myself in something slightly more offensive than glory.

There are bad responses to invitations to a night out and there are also horrendous farty ones, you know the real stinkers like, "my beloved dog Kenneth is ill" your Nan also works fine for this, "its's Easter Monday tomorrow" and my favourite "you know I would love to but I just can't".

Then there are excuses that are in a league of their own, these are the lonely Gary ones the real revenge of the albatross type, the ones women use when unattractive men with suspect stains in the groin area of their trousers approach them in a bar, the real "fuck off fatty" ones (given that I shouldn't really be allowed out on my own sometimes) you will have by now guessed that I went all the way to Twattytown with my response, and I admit now that I didn't have a return ticket and at this point I should have gone directly to jail and not collected two hundred pounds and I should have applied for instant euthanasia, in fact I would go so far as to say that I would have been better off setting myself on fire and jumping out of a closed window screaming (I wish I had been that clever) I'm ashamed to say I shambled out the world's worst response in the history of not only dating but also mankind, not "mate is that piss on your trousers" but the old wanky favourite "I'll check my diary and come back to you" damn my poor brain, damn that microchip and bugger me to hell, what an idiot! to this day I can't believe how incredibly close I came to messing things up and in hindsight I would have preferred my arse to have exploded because at least then I could have claimed a medical emergency and had could have excused myself and sought refuge at the local casualty unit. I may have well shit on the desk.

Undeterred Michaela offered me her phone number and walked off into the distance to meet and marry the man of her dreams, I watched her leave knowing that I had taken the coward's way out. I had avoided the last awkward goodbye and by the time she would realize I wasn't coming to her night out I would be miles away, a far and distant memory to her. She would never know that I really did love her enough to let her go. What would a homecoming queen want with this old daydream believer anyway?

The following day I busied myself with preparations to leave, I tidied the house and made sure that everything was in its place. I looked through old family photographs and recounted happier times, uncles, and aunts no longer with us smiling into the camera at my sister's twenty first birthday party many years before. I safely tucked away my memories into little boxes in my mind and stored my photos back into their little blue box. The grief of losing mum hit me again, life felt heavy and was well and truly on top of me.

I was taken back to a time on the Isle of Wight a few months earlier when I knew my mum was ill and although it was never said I understood then that she was dying. I was standing at the sink in the kitchen watching my mum in the conservatory through the window. She was doing what she always had done, she was pottering around adjusting throws on the settee and straightening the cushions, I was zapped back to my childhood home, my head spun and the images of mum and I doing the washing and other menial household tasks together washed over me, I never thought memories of such simple tasks could bring me so much pleasure, I remember following her around as she went about her day happily letting me help.

I was always a mummy's boy and I would drive her mad sometimes with my incessant need for her attention, often she would escape into the bathroom just to get a little space from me only to emerge later to find me encamped outside the toilet door with my toy cars and a great big smile It was our version of Troy only better because my mum was playing. I loved her completely and she was my world.

I smiled at my mum as I washed up soon bought back to earth by geese calling overhead, mum just being there was comforting, it was familiar like an old raincoat or a taxi in the rain. When I was little I believed that my mum would be around forever, the concept that she wouldn't was all too much for me to bare then as it is now and as I returned to the present I had sharp engulfing pangs of fear that my childhood was ending, we were in the autumn of something big and all I could do was watch and watch I did, so intently, recording in my mind every movement, every nuance and every second. I wanted to force myself to remember her; I wanted it pressed so firm in my mind that it would be impossible for me to forget her. I still have this abiding memory of her now, busying herself making sure all was right and balanced in the world that everyone was comfortable and had what they needed. Occasionally I berate myself for such a cowardly act.

I once sat with mum at the dining room table, reassuring myself that she wasn't going to die, I sat happily writing down the ages that she would be and the ages that I would be at certain stages of our lives, "when I'm seven, you will be twenty seven, when I'm twenty you will be forty" in my naivety I soon arrived at mum's hundred and sixth birthday by which time I'd be a spritely eighty six and ready to consider living without mum, I remember distinctly a lump forming in my throat when I got to sixty six, mum jokingly said "I'll be in my box by then!" the very idea buckled me at the knees, I instantly began to cry, mum gathered me up in her arms and gave me a hug "only joking" she chimed, That day imprinted itself in my mind and how I wish it was just a joke as the reality of things set in, I remember everything about that moment, the way she was dressed and the way she gently squeezed me close". I longed to be squeezed again.

I was ready for my travels by early evening, I would worry where I was going on Monday when I woke up, for now I was preparing a Saturday night in, I had bought myself the Charlie Chaplin masterpiece the Kid on DVD, I loved this film, the pathos was baked right in and almost instant.

The kid seemed appropriate and as I settled into the film, I realised that this would potentially be the last time I would sit in my familiar chair surrounded by familiar things in the home that I had worked so hard to build. As I sat big fat tears rolled once again down my face, at first a gentle stream but soon keenly followed by big hot, fat real tears, I was broken I related to Chaplin as he was forever the Orphan, a man trying to do good in a world that was stacked against him. A man of frustration, at odds with the world but not embittered by it, in Chaplin I saw myself. If only I had his genius.

Soon a tired energy washed over me, the effort to hand over the reins at work, the constant goodbyes, sans the most important one and the organisation for my trip took its toll, I felt heavy, old, and alone. Sleep washed over me until I was bought crashing down to earth with a thud, the sounding of what I thought was thunder followed by a crash that I later understood to be a relatively well controlled explosion.

Mum it seems had other plans for me that night, as I came to my senses a deafening silence surrounded me. I had no power, no light, and no clue. After scrabbling about in my garage using an assortment of swear words instead of tools I hit upon the problem, the fuse box had blown and taken the breaker panel out with it. In short, I was now sat in the middle of the creek without a paddle. The only way I was getting power back was if my mum descended from heaven with a team of late (aren't they always) electricians, I mean if an electrician was on time I would be more in awe of that miracle than the resurrection that Christ, but for now I was limited to this realm and with a huge sigh I resigned myself to a night in the cold and dark, if only I had somewhere to be.

I jumped into my car and within an hour I arrived at the Kings Head Hornchurch, I steeled myself and drank in the heavy atmosphere, a mixture of beer and cigarette smoke engulfed me, even with my vision swimming through the palls of smoke, I saw her, I stopped and drank her in, a band was playing in the garden I stood by the speakers, the noise cloaked me, I could walk away now and preserve myself, bottle my feelings and move on. I turned to walk when mum in one last desperate attempt to clip me round the ear send a blast of feedback through the speaker I was standing next to in an instant the whole pub turned to face me uttering a single chorus of fuck me! As the ringing in my ears cut through my skull our eyes met, she smiled, and I walked towards her.

Michaela and I had spoken for hours after we met that fateful night, we spoke at length about ourselves with real honesty, I told Michaela about my mum and the grief that I felt, she told me about her unhappy relationship that had ended some time ago. We were two lost souls that in some way had connected, we had found each other. At first it was hard for me to explain to Michaela just how lovely she was to me. She encouraged me to talk openly to her. It felt natural to have her all around me, the chilly grip of loneliness that had engulfed me for so long was gone, I knew then that although our path would not always run smooth our love always would. To this day it is still the only thing I can count on for certain.

We talked into the small hours, the conversation. A story for another time, for now though here I was on the cusp of a new relationship and a new chapter of my life about to begin. Michaela understood my grief and I explained my plan, I told her my plans for running away from home and that I really needed to take time out for myself, I had been working full time for almost twenty years without one day of unemployment. I had always done the right thing, the sensible thing. I had been paying my rent, bills, and taxes since I was seventeen.

I had foregone foreign holidays with friends as I never money for them, they all lived with their parents and had money that was as disposable as their jobs. I was different. I had to work. I was on my own. I never felt I missed out but now I felt decidedly rebellious. This was something that had built inside of me for all those years; losing mum was the preverbal straw that broke the camel's back. I was compelled to go. I said goodbye to Michaela on the Sunday evening wishing that I could have had her for longer. I asked her in vein to come with me, a foolhardy enterprise of a man who for the first time in his life was being selfish. I knew she couldn't and I felt ashamed to have asked her, I remember her response as if it was yesterday, her face was set in stone, she looked at me, her look was intense "where are we going?" my mind raced with all the possibilities this great country offered, my mind was filled with long and winding roads, red pillar boxes, telegraph poles and the long-forgotten telephone boxes. My heart sang with thoughts of the English seaside, the Donald McGill postcard and Carry on films.

This was to be a once in a lifetime road trip, it had no end and at present it still more importantly had no beginning, which when you are running away from home is no small matter. I thought of the people I had met along the way to this point, some you will hear about, others saved for another day.

Soon my thoughts turned to days gone by, the nit nurse at school, the smell of the classroom and the freshly mowed grass in the fields beyond. The age of innocence. Life seemed so much better then, an illusion almost. I was resolute in my answer, the simple realisation dawned Michaela and I had a lifetime to share "where are we going?" I mused, the answer clear and simple as could be, in an instant I replied" back to the start".

Chapter four: the future falls from a tree

We arrived at our first stop fifteen minutes after we left home, my childhood home stood before me. The road was the same eclectic mix of cars and vans parked to varying standards of competency by their respective owners, although there was more of them now, I appreciated how much the road had shrunk, I had vivid memories of long summers spent here running breathlessly from one end of the street to the other this was my world back then. I remembered fondly my mum stood on the pavement in the sunshine dividing this little empire, our corner of England into segments of the places I could and couldn't go, stood in this little urban street more than thirty years later I recalled the clear instructions, a decree by my mum it was I now thought (with my adult trousers on) like Hitler stood before his literal captive audience on a dais proclaiming territorial rights. My mum's however unlike Hitler merely extended to the end of each of the next-door neighbour's garden boundaries. This wasn't twelve-inch banner headline stuff it was as it turns out to be the peripheral lines of vision afforded from our kitchen window.

These solemn proclamations (she also was not for turning) was reinforced by truly confounding home spun urban myths designed to terrify us into never leaving her domain. The most frightening of all was what lay behind Mrs Snubblupicas' wall at the end of the street (Snubblupicas was not her real name this was a name afforded to her years later by my school friend Danny Scutts due to her remarkable resemblance to an elephant like Sesame street character but that is a different story for another day) It was something so truly terrifying that it could push anyone to their psychological limit, it wasn't something not of this earth, nor a man propelled across the universe by no horse drawn it was much more sinister, much more macabre, something that until this day has never been written about.

You see for this siren, this heap of malevolence was none other than a man of the normal variety (you may need to use your imagination here, try placing yourself in the mind of a slightly neurotic five year old and his not quite switched on friend and you will get the gist) not missing anything in terms of body parts and on the flip side he had no additional appendages either (no extra eyes, claws or teeth) in fact he didn't even have any sweeties and there was not one puppy in sight and as far as we ever knew he was completely without a van.

This hooded claw as myth told us was nothing more terrifying than a man sat behind the wall in the middle of the road, taking his shoes and socks off and to this end we were all bloody terrified (the fact there was no road to sit in beyond the wall hadn't yet computed in my adolescent brain).

Rumour had it that he would remain there all day until all the children were safely in bed when he would then hoist an aging radio cassette player on to his shoulders and would walk the streets listening to capitol radio while lamenting that he wished radio one would close down as capitol radio was king. (I often wondered if he put his shoes and socks back on to do this). I always wondered if he had a knocking off time, maybe a formal agreement, did his supervisor ring him up "when the streetlights come on mate you can go home as all the little buggers will be indoors, no that's ok you can leave your stuff there until tomorrow, yes mate I'll keep an eye on it", or was it a go with your instincts type of arrangement. I still wonder about that now on a slow Wednesday afternoon when I should be working.

In hindsight this scene pretty much describes Catford High Street on any given afternoon perhaps now though times have moved on and I think that this fabled depraved child worrier in this day and age would have a water tight contract, transactional based schedule, a 48 hour directive working opt out form and a copy of the equality act all rolled up in his stripy (villains always have striped socks) little cotton socks bless him, but back then to my five-year-old self I was satisfied enough that these lines should not be crossed and I never dared to venture too far. It just goes to show mums really do know best!

As I stood there reminiscing about a world that no longer existed I felt sadness creeping up behind me, Michaela hung back as I walked down the street my thoughts and memories gathered momentum, Michaela had seen me several times withdraw into myself and as if by magic she always seemed to know the best thing to do for me, sometimes it was best to let me go. She got me from day one that is why I love her so much.

 It was now almost thirty years since I had left this place and its bogey men behind but I was all too aware that I now had other demons, my mind raced with them after all that was why I was now stood here running away from one home only to seek out another. My childhood played out before me, in this vista the sun was hotter, the ice creams were bigger, and my mum was stood at the kitchen window surveying her territorial claim watching over me. I always knew back then that everything would be alright because she was there.

 I was compelled to follow the road towards the bottom end of the street the neat little houses stood attention and passed muster, in my mind I drifted back to the great garage fire of 81, when during one of those long hot summers that we are no longer allowed to enjoy due to the greenhouse effect or just in case anyone accidentally gets sexually harassed in the process, the residents of the street were in their front gardens enjoying the sounds of ABBA that were floating in the air along with the smells of old Holborn, cigarette smoke and slightly warm lager.

Several of the larger neighbours had since vacated their gardens in favour of a quick run to the local hospital after sitting in a 1970's style plastic lawn chair left over from the queen's silver jubilee street party celebrations that had undoubtedly eaten one or both of their testicles, this was a well-known risk in 1980's Britain many men have been taken away in an ambulance with the chair still attached to their undercarriage ably supported by a slightly tired wife with a look of divorce in her eyes, only a fool or a drunk would sit in a chair of this construct without thoroughly checking it for cracks, it is a simple but fatally overlooked process that can be achieved easily by pushing firmly in the centre of the chair with the palm of your hand while checking for movement along any suspect cracks, without this inspection even a small hairline fracture may seem benign that is until body weight is applied then you have the full on jaws scenario as the alligator teeth of the chair takes a chunk out of an unsuspecting gonad or two, the chair will gently take any right or left dressed low hanging fruit into its mouth unnoticed cutting feeling and blood supply until the unwitting victim is ready to get up causing the jaws spring shut trapping everything within generating much screaming and amusement depending on how sympathetic your friends are which is a mere prelude to the relief of a blackout (I learned over many years that while the victim is enjoying the blackout, prone and vulnerable is by far the best time to yank the chair off the victim and put him in the recovery position or draw a penis on said victim's face) this is why the visual inspection of a chair will never do and only a divorced one balled fool with a pained squint will tell you otherwise!

I'm still not sure if this is where the term plum derived from, referring to the colour of said testicle after a visit to the hospital with the dreaded lawn chair attached to your wife's wedding present when someone slips into the vernacular but it may be just a happy coincidence.

I digressed then, however back to my point one of the garages from the block at the end of the street had caught fire and as quick as kindling it proceeded to ignite the surrounding units,(the garage owner Smokey Vic who had a passion for chain smoking and flicking cigarette ends for Follie had no idea how this started, the fact he was covered in soot and was dragged out the garage still holding an empty bottle of scotch at the time of the fire was merely a happenstance) as the fire made it's was towards the houses (in a quiet and orderly fashion please, no running!) a team of highly unskilled and slightly inebriated residents (or our dads as we knew them) immediately sprang into action but unlike the fire they were less orderly, less organised and to be honest slightly outwitted. It was like watching a shitty episode of the keystone cops.

The men of the street soon showed their character, my dad was beaming from ear to ear as he loved a crisis, there was Bill who was my friend Danny's dad moving his car from the melee (it was the only posh one in the street) we had Pete the ambulance driver fresh from a chair run to Orpington hospital advising everyone to leave it to "his colleagues" the professionals, (I think he was the first person down our street to say the word colleague, very posh) the rest of the group threw themselves into disorganised chaos heaving buckets of water at the fire only to have it evaporate on impact. I remember the sense of community even at that young age, I looked upon this scene of a community coming together, and I remember being overwhelmed and thinking, what dickheads but they were my dickheads. I am sad that this spirit of community has disappeared from our streets and that our lives are becoming more and more isolated and solitary and the sadder part is that our children won't have these first-hand experiences and stories to tell their children. Storytelling like the art of joke telling is fading away giving over to the simple cold act of texting, shame.

As I neared the end of the road I made my way towards checkpoint Charlie, the wall of no return to the side of Mrs Snubblupicas' house

I still felt compelled to check that a barefoot man was not lurking, I remembered the time my mum put on my sisters blue and yellow roller boots that were all the rage lethally dangerous and absolutely naff but at the same time the envy of every child, and proceeded to head in the direction I was now in, stopping only very briefly as she bounced over the bonnet of a shitty Datsun and landed on the other side, I remember her laughter ringing out as we ran towards her to see if she was in need of an ambulance, as I arrived at the scene I gazed over the bonnet of the car I realized that on the other side of the Datsun was a pretty steep drop that was broken only by a mountain of compost and debris that luckily had broken mum's fall but not her spirit, all can still hear her now through fits of giggles shouting "get me my shoes!", as the wan sun danced across my face I replayed this wonderful memory over and over in my mind, the Datsun was long gone as were many of the families that had once lived here when this small little street was my world.

The road looked different now, trees and gardens had given way to paved or tarmacked parking spaces, cars were now crammed wherever they could be squeezed, all that remained of the green spaces was the a place we called the ramp, this was because the green stood at the base of a long hill where we would take turns to try and kill ourselves by going down the hill sat on a skateboard and hitting the sloped mound that would carry us onto the grass, if you were lucky physics would kick in and slow you down enough to avoid hitting the road, luck would stop you hitting the wall and skill was the only thing left between you and your god. if you was very lucky you would miss the tree planted firmly if not a little defiantly just to the left of the ramp, the dream though for all of us was to clear the green completely and reach the road with enough skill that you could stop before you caved your head in on the then infamous Datsun (remembering back then that any form of safety equipment was not only frowned upon but thought to be completely girlie) the use of one left you open to all manner of farmyard animal noises, limp wristed gestures and chants of "spazamaroonee" and at the time we all thought that a good job too!

As I now stood against the tree remembering the time my friend Ben got stuck up the tree after a botched boy scout impression whereby it turned out they didn't teach tree climbing in the scouts, we found this to be true as it transpired that A: Ben was not in the scouts and B: Ben was petrified of heights, so after panicked minutes of discussion and much cat calling (our favourites at the time were the tried and tested "spazamaroonee" and thanks to a recent episode of Blue Peter there was a craze to shout "hello I'm a Joey, I'm Joey Deacon" after some poor bastard that was being wheeled out on national television in the name of fund raising). Ben decided he would rather take the risk of jumping out of the tree than have us watching from ground zero going to fetch his mum.

You may think it strange that jumping out of a tree rather than having your loving mum help you down and kiss it all better was the final defiant act of a desperate man, but I must draw your attention to some learned behaviour, only a few weeks previous to tree gate Ben had had a fantastic idea of riding his skateboard down the slide at the local park, there was two problems with this (that had been calculated, four further issues surfaced after the point of no return) venture being that this was 1980 something and the fun police were still a way off into the future and our little gang lacked any serious grasp of risk assessments. We soon came to the conclusion that a skateboard would easily bounce upon landing on grass and would gently come to a stop by its own volition we didn't think any further about safety enhancements for fear of the enterprise being considered girly which would be the height of social suicide. This enterprise, this proud moment for our gang was going to be a main feature on par with Evil Kinevil, everything felt right, and Ben was set to show the world how brave we all were.

The problems however, were there from the start, to be fair it really was science that day that let us down that day and as Ben sat on his skateboard atop the slide he released his grip for the decent, He panicked as momentum shifted and Ben made a one handed desperate grab for the side of the slide this unfortunately sent him into a brilliant spin (this was a true ten out of ten although more for style than grace) he continued his now unplanned and quite surprising backwards decent down the slide where we met with problem number two, the gang's technical advisors hadn't planned for the slight upturned end of the slide designed to slow a graceful decent in normal circumstances, which now given the velocity of the skateboard and the weight of the user had now caused Ben to unexpectedly alight the ride in one direction while the skateboard took a different course, the next two problems are now bought in to play, problem three was that in true NASA style part of the skateboard (the rear set of wheels) had broken away from the rest of the board and were now independent so as the rest of Ben's board went one way with Ben pissing off in the other and coming to land a few feet ahead of the end of the slide which as it turned out proved to be a brilliant launch pad for a set of skateboard wheels that were following at a good speed which proceeded to smack Ben straight in the back of the head at the exact moment problem number four (or Ben's mum as she was known) turned the corner of the road. She had witnessed this ballet of Follie.

Upon seeing we had a man down situation, we were relieved to see her, or at least everyone except Ben was, as she came running towards him I thought in a mother's grief for her fallen hero but as she neared I could see murder in her eyes as she grabbed Ben's skateboard from its final resting place and expertly broke the remains over her knee (to a spontaneous exclamation of oh shit from the rest of the gang) and as she met with Ben's dazed, diluted and slightly damp eyes she expertly assessed the situation quickly determining that he had not suffered enough and with that she picked him up to his feet, held him in the air and began to beat him while rhythmically berating him in time to the slaps, to her credit even as she began to tire and run out of words with which to chide him she split each word into syllables and smacked on each.

It was therefore decided that as Ben sat in the tree stranded it would be my mum that would be the one to come and help us, she soon arrived and expertly assessed the situation and soon had Ben down and smiling, her kindness bought Ben to tears, she helped him as we all walked to our house her arm gently draped around his shoulders.

 Minutes later we were sat in the front room of our house eating ice cream and planning our next adventure. That you see was mum. This was perhaps the best result, a few weeks early big Glen one of the older boys had been climbing the tree and with egotistical gusto had launched himself from one of the branches, tragically he forgot to bend his knees upon being reunited with the ground biting the end of his tongue and winding himself, after some tears and a snotty nose he was collected by his mum and after a short ambulance ride it was established that he had fractured his ankle and Dawn from round the corner's collar bone. She had been the object of his affection and the recipient of his adolescent showing off, unfortunately she was perched on his landing strip and was taken out in the melee. Dawn went off Glen after that which was a good thing as any attempt at French kissing would have been impossible given that glen was missing the best bit of his tongue.

 I was blessed having the cool, kind and popular mum, she was the mum that respected us and let us find our way, she never judged and was always the mum that everybody told the truth to, this pattern of compassion played out many times over the years in many ways and to many people which is why my mum is known as "the Mumma" to all my friends and to all of my three sister's friends too. It was at times of remembrance like these that always proved too much for me to bare, these were the chilly moments when I knew I would miss her forever, these were when I hated Cancer the most. This is what made me so angry, with anger though comes love and love for me has always won out, I can't help but wish that we all could have had Mumma for longer.

There are so many childhood memories that flood back to me and I often share them with my son, I love that even though he is a teenager he will still sit for hours laughing at the stories I tell about how I shambled from one disaster to another. He suggested once that I should write a book about it, I think one day I might.

My childhood was perfect, idyllic some would say. I was pained by the realisation that this little corner of England and mum was gone. This was my past, where I had come from. I was a little boy again, I wondered if I should have wandered so far from home. I was a runaway (albeit a 36-year-old one) I was all too aware that mum wouldn't be able to see me from the window anymore and her guiding hand was gone, this seemed all too surreal to me now, I felt Michaela's hand on my shoulder. I knew it was time to go.

Chapter Five: All is fair in love and war!

Michaela and I headed south on the M20 for Dover, we chose Dover as the starting point for our adventure because I had spent time here on holiday with my mum and my sisters and in the years that followed I had become nostalgic about the place and now I was keen to show Michaela the sites of some of my greatest family arguments and fallings out.

One such time I remember fondly had culminated one hot summer evening when my sister Cheryl found while walking along the front in Dover an plush doll from an old 1980's children's program called Rainbow Sprite (yes it was really as bad as you image) The doll was in the image of the protagonist's arch enemy Murky Dismal, as soon as Cheryl had picked the doll up my other sister Beccy claimed that it was her that found Murky and from that moment on the whole evening of our holiday was spent arguing until my aunt Viv propositioned that the doll was probably cursed anyway and that in all probability it had been abandoned that very night by some other poor long suffering family that had suffered a similar fate resulting in the undoubted death of the doll's finder, adequately spooked Murky was soon consigned to the next nearest bin, suitably freaked out Cheryl lowered Murky into the bin (for what we hoped for the sake of all children would be the last time) as she did so I heard her mutter "fuck that shit", the strange thing was as soon as Murky was gone everyone stopped arguing! this was Viv's gift she was eccentric and ballsy enough to pull off some of the best home spun bullshit and make it as believable as the law and to all us kids her word was gospel, it's that power that she had that endears her to me to this day many years after her death, she was that aunt. It was in the spirit of adventure and the promise of a story that we headed south to Viv's own country.

We would holiday in Dover and the surrounding areas of Margate, Ramsgate and beyond as my aunt Viv and my uncle Dennis had moved to Deal (an upscale hamlet outside Dover) in the mid 1980's and the opportunity for cheap escapes to seaside was too good an opportunity to pass up (even if we were sometimes subjected to what could only be described as institutional type cuisine) money for us back then was incredibly tight and Dover was our only real option of a holiday. There was only ever one scandal in terms of the cooking and it came unintentionally from my sister Cheryl who was overheard by Viv remarking that "the dinner tonight was truly shitty in the finest tradition of the seaside doss house" (Cheryl was 10 at the time). Viv who could be a little highly strung at times (she had been known to get very worked up about the price of carrots) had to be unstrung by my mum after the dinner gate scandal with large quantities of diplomacy and whiskey that seemed to do the trick (the whiskey, not the diplomacy) well at least it seemed to as Viv was placated enough that she found strength in her heart to make an attempt to sit on my uncle Dennis' knee while singing a selection of what I can only describe as Bawdy wartime songs (I could tell by the scowl on Dennis' face that he loved every minute of it), however Crisis on this occasion was averted, my mum the alcohol wielding Politician had triumphed. I sometimes think if she was alive now, we could have sent her to the EU negotiations with a selection of fine spirits, a few packs of fags and within a few hours the whole thing would be sorted out with everyone agreeing to play nicely.

My uncle Dennis was a proud sea faring man like me (but in very different circumstances also ran away from home) Dennis was 14 at the time and fled a starkly different childhood to mine, He was sold by his birth mother to one of her relatives so that a council house could be purloined by way of the totally unnecessary adoption, this was Britain in the 1930's and it all seems just too awful. Dennis never really got over the betrayal, although in his later years he managed to have a functional relationship with his mum, as much as one can try and move on from that I don't think it is ever something you can.

Dennis and Viv moved to Dover when Dennis became an officer working for the Dover Harbour authority working on the Tug boats bringing the large cruise and cargo ships into port, He had decided to abstain from deep sea sailing and made a concerted effort build a life on the land, this he managed for 18 months before the lure of the ocean took him, he ended his career as a commissioned officer on the luxury cruise ships most notable of these was the Canberra (on which he proudly sailed to the Falkland Islands during the conflict).

Dennis as a run-away first became a submariner, then a Navy man for many years eventually joining the merchant navy which opened up the world to him and aunt Viv, they travelled extensively around the world, although Dennis never spoke much about his adventures one of his greatest played out at to me at his funeral in 2005, Dennis sadly died 3 months after his retirement asbestosis from years on the merchant ships did for him, He collected exactly one week of state pension after a lifetime of contributing to his country.

 It was a beautiful July day St George's Church on the Deal seafront seemed to be the perfect location to say goodbye to Dennis, it overlooked the sea and was peaceful, the church was bathed in glorious sunlight and the summer air made us feel glad to be alive, the smell of fresh cut grass made me close my eyes and briefly I was transported back to my childhood., I have always found that the smell of cut grass and the sound of the workmen strimming the hedges and the banks takes me back to my old infant school and for a moment I am a child again.

I soon shifted from my reverie as the hearse arrived, we dutifully filed into the church behind the impressive gold trimmed coffin. The service music played (sailing by Rod Stewart of course) and we took our seats, my eyes wandered through the rows of neatly turned out mourners, I thought to myself that Primark must have taken a battering and as I supressed a giggle I took in the nautical themed stained-glass windows and the religious trinkets scattered throughout the church, I'm not a religious person and the awe I expect was lost on me but my eyes were drawn to a group of people sat at the back of the church, I knew if not personally but by name everyone present but throughout the service as much as I tried I just didn't recognise them. I assumed they were visiting the church and had inadvertently got caught up in our service and had failed to escape before the dreaded site of the pall bearer bore down on them, I thought how funny Dennis would find this, a group of middle aged people minding their own business had come to his funeral by mistake. I soon admonished myself for smiling while the vicar was walking in the Valley of death (Dartford I presume).

I arrived at the cemetery in Hamilton Road just ahead of the hearse and I detoured slightly to pay my respects to three now forgotten heroes, Hamilton Road has a military history and is attached to the Deal Barracks that tragically was bombed by the IRA in 1989, 11 serviceman were killed that day and in terrible sadness I stood at the graves of Robert Nolan aged 21, Patrick Povey aged 31 and Timothy Petch aged 26 they being the most recent and I pray the last military service personnel killed on duty to be buried here. Surrounded by the great and good I knew I was in good company; I saw mum beckoning me I hurried towards what would be Dennis' last resting place.

The finite details of the day are now long since washed from my memory, the wake was held at my aunt's house and my mum was busy making tea and unwrapping various plates of food (mum was always great in a crisis or in fact whenever you needed her to be great) it's when I reflect back on times that these that I feel angry with her for leaving me It hurts in the most profound and gut wrenching way, Mother's day, birthdays and Christmas I can cope with now but in times of trouble or doubt I really struggle.

It's odd when someone you love dies as you start counting the days since they left you, then you count the weeks, the months and the anniversaries but after a while you find yourself starting to count the times when you need them, that's when the anger comes.

I was once asked a question by my good and oldest friend Danny, the question being if I could spend an hour sat on bench talking to anyone either living or dead who would I choose, I mulled this over and replied anyone but my mum, you see an hour with my mum wouldn't be long enough, I couldn't face seeing her go again, in fact I would cause a scene reminiscent of a child leaving his mum at the school gate for the first time, this much I know couldn't say goodbye a second time. Kicking and screaming I would be torn from her loving embrace, my ears would burst to hear her soft and gentle voice again and my soul would die a thousand times to feel the gentle pat of her hand on mind, part of love is loss, this sentiment is true but it sucks. Anger is the most difficult part of grief, it has been for me the hardest thing to tame, to be honest I'm not even sure if I have.

Soon after the small chit chat had started and the tea had begun to flow the mystery group from the service appeared at the door, greeted by my aunt she said "It's lovely to see you, Dennis would be so proud to see you all" I asked them how they knew my uncle Dennis, I wasn't entirely prepared for their answer but within half an hour I wished that I had known Dennis better.

The six now middle-aged men and women were students travelling in the middle east in the 1970's they had stopped at the same hotel where Dennis and Viv were also staying, shortly after their arrival there was an insurgent rebellion and the hotel was invaded by terrorists and the few guests that remained at the hotel now found themselves to be hostages, they were cut off from civilian and allied forces and the surrounding area soon became a minefield as political unrest soon spread.

Dennis took the six youngsters under his wing and made sure that that they got fed and watered, after a week the tensions were growing in the area and air strikes commenced, gunfire had become almost normal, Dennis was an extremely clever man and knew that the group didn't have much time and he needed to take a calculated risk, he didn't tell the frightened teens then that they were facing certain death, that he kept to himself.

One morning Dennis disappeared for a while announcing that he was going for a swim in the now abandoned swimming pool and that Viv should go and get their now adopted six teenage children and meet him poolside, after a while Dennis settled everyone down in a quiet corner of the pool area, then calmly as one of the captors passed him he barged him to the ground and expertly hit him on the side of his head with the butt of a rifle, he took the gun, faced his follow captives and said "follow me, don't run, don't turn round. Get straight into the back of the truck and lay down, do not move or speak until I tell you".

With that Dennis set off through a small door and ushered Viv and children into the back of a truck (to this day nobody knows where he got this from), all Viv could do was to keep repeating what Dennis had told them over and over, "don't look back, Don't look back" soon they were safely in the back of truck, as instructed they laid down, Dennis took a white towel on which he had daubed a crude red cross symbol, and he draped it over the front of the truck, Gunfire erupted both from the direction of the hotel and from the cab of the truck as the truck sped off, soon Dennis was driving through the warzone, laced with mines and god knows what other terrible tools of war and for what seemed like hours Viv and the teenagers lay face down in the truck with only their respective gods and darkness for company, over the cracking of gun fire, they felt every movement of the old rickety truck, every trench, every crater and rattle was a step closer to freedom until eventually the truck stopped and the quiet engulfed them. They could just about over their heartbeats hear Dennis speaking but couldn't work out what he was saying, then as if like thunder and a crack of lightening the truck doors opened and stood next to Dennis were 3 British Airforce Guards, they had made it.

After a day or so the Teenagers said their goodbyes to my uncle and aunt as they flew home on board a RAF plane, they were safe. My uncle returned to business as usual and along with my aunt re-joined his ship. The events of that day and the silence on board the truck had followed Dennis to his grave.

The six-people stood before me now were those teenagers, they were in no doubt that they owed their lives and the lives of their own children to my Uncle Dennis, I think back now and realise just how much I loved visiting Dover and the South-East coast, I also realised how much I loved him. Having a guy like Dennis as your holiday guide was always going to be an adventure. A great man in every way and one that aspire to be like every day.

As I focused on the road I remembered a story about my aunt Viv that always made me and mum laugh, Viv was driving from our house in Orpington back home to Deal, as she entered the M20 she wound the window down to enjoy the breeze and was soon on the receiving end of many funny glances from other road users combined with a few surprising honks on the horn from various motorists. She even had a barrage of cat calls and whistles from the army trucks full of soldiers as she passed them.

Viv was completely bemused by this prospect, to be fair she was bemused much of the time which was a condition I always attributed to a rather large German bomb exploding in close proximity to her at the time of her birth and giving off a cloud of stupid gas, or more likely the Kaboom got the better of her mother's nerves causing her to drop the newly arrived bundle of joy!

Given that Viv was in her new car (it was a bog standard little metro that shouldn't really garner much attention) however un phased and feeling groovy Viv decided it was her brand new shiny car that was getting the attention (she must have been dropped surely?) but as she got to the end of the M20 at Dover and turned on to the Jubilee way towards Deal and she was even more confused to be getting cheers from the various work men accompanied by many double thumbs up, they really were a patriotic bunch she thought as she passed by with all these people admiring her decision to buy British! but sadly as she pulled up on to her driveway Viv soon discovered it was more peeping Tom than patriotism that had caused scenes of merry England that had not been seen since Charles married Diana, as alas the mystery was soon solved by Viv's neighbour a kindly old gentleman who between stifled laughs pointed out that Viv had suffered what would nowadays be known as a wardrobe malfunction of the Janet Jackson variety, she had started the day in an elasticated strapless dress sans bra which had as she wound the window down buggered off from her chest area and settled nicely below her chest. She had been a moving peep show for best part of fifty miles, Viv was never one to be deterred and I am reliably informed that this was not the first nor the last time that this happened, I only wish that it hadn't happened again one blustery day in front of my friend Richard Peters and me at the top of Dover castle one summer holiday, It was like 2 torpedo missiles coming at us only twice as frightening, no wonder he spent the rest of that holiday wetting the bed.

Full of the memories of long forgotten summers we pulled into dover and soon we were headed for the western heights a favourite place of mine on the outcrop of Dover harbour, right upon the white cliffs of dover, I have been an avid urban explorer for many years but this place with its views over the English channel out to France and its famous history always makes me return, I was surprised to learn that the Seven Sisters cliffs all the way down the coast in East Sussex (where I now live) are actually the Iconic cliffs that appear as the white cliffs of dover in many TV and film productions as they are far more unspoilt by war and industry, but for me these true cliffs with their proud history are a sight for sore eyes.

We walked along the old casements the sun shone down on us, the smell of the summer rain drying out in the grass and the steady breeze made for a heady mix. The casements were placed here in 194X as an anti-aircraft installation. The guns now long gone have made way for a beautiful coastal walk along the heights.

The original earthworks were formed in 1779 with the larger Drop Redoubt first works phase starting in 1804 to 1808 as the war with Napoleon raged on around it, after a review request from the royal commission further expansion was completed between 1859 and 1864.

But now the once a busy and thriving military installation now lays quiet, the harsh brick and cobbled court yards have given way to the beautiful flowers that adorn every inch of the heights from wild orchids to the sycamore trees everything here grows in resplendent beauty. To my left as I looked across the cliffs I spotted the forever reliable outline of Dover castle and to the front of me towards the channel itself Archcliffe Fort looked back at me, daring any would be invader to have a go and as I looked around our abandoned military heritage that lay before me it reminded me what was and what could have so easily been.

The air was heavy and still, the salty mix of the sea mingled with the flowers and grass and as we walked up the steep verges away from the casements towards the Drop redoubt I felt brave, ready for adventures new almost like the soldiers that had walked here hundreds of years before me, looking towards the unknown, feeling a mixed sense of dread laced with excitement. My journey was not going to need the courage that the soldiers needed nor would it be as defining but the experiences I was about to have and the muster which I had to call upon was no less trite.

Thoughts of the journeys that lay ahead filled me with hope; after all I had a beautiful lady with me to my future and only the past behind me. I felt no fear of what was to come. Every direction led me away from home, but to me this all made sense and several times I tried to vocalize these feelings to Michaela, but my words were too poor and my sentiments too high to coherently explain. I sensed that she knew however and as she squeezed my hand, I squeezed through the low hanging and extremely claustrophobic tunnel towards the drop redoubt itself.

As we cleared the tunnel the drop fort stood before us a breath-taking feat of engineering, now a gentle and almost secret nature reserve that had vowed never to reveal its secrets; this is a peaceful place and as Michaela and I sat and rested in the sun, our surroundings as English as a post box we refreshed our hungry bellies with pork pies and ham sandwiches. Time passed and feeling rested I closed my eyes as I lay on the dry grass, as stretched out as the sounds of the sea in my mind washed over me and I was transported back to long hot summers playing on the beach below the cliffs with my mum and sisters. We were all present, but never correct. It was a fine roll call including my cousins, aunts and uncles all reporting for duty. A real family affair.

I recalled a time (in colour) of mum sitting although sitting may be too generous a word may attempting to sit on one of my aunt's cheap deck chairs, you know the type, the ones covered in horrible flowers with a liberal scattering of some horrible chickens (or birds of paradise as my aunt referred to them) anyway these chairs were old and dangerous (Viv was famous for giving away old things that was invariably a little worse for ware and extremely dangerous) I recalled the time she gave me and my sister an old iron (not any old iron) when we moved into our first house, I was happily ironing away one evening blissfully happy and completely unaware that I had managed to iron my entire wardrobe (two shirts, one pair of jeans) without having the device plugged in when Cheryl spotted the flaw and ever so helpfully plugged the iron in which then instantly exploded into flames taking the ironing board, my entire wardrobe and part of my left eyebrow with it. Cheryl reacted very fast and shot out the room with her handbag to get me something to fight the fire with, or so I thought. After several minutes which seemed like hours (these things do when all your worldly possessions are in flames) I realised that Cheryl was sans help, after putting out the blaze using a skilfully balanced combination of water, psychology and violence I reminded myself to write Viv a note thanking her for the experience if not for the iron.

As I run cold water over my half an eyelash I looked up from the sink and through the kitchen window I saw Cheryl outside well beyond the looking glass and indeed the boundary of our house having evacuated herself from the scene moments earlier, she was now leaning against a corporation lamp post waiting patiently for the all clear. Sometimes the smoke really does get in your eyes and right up your arse at the same time. With Viv it was like the ritual a bride would follow, something old, something new, something borrowed, something blue only for us the mantra was more straight forward as we followed the Viv mantra of something dangerous, something to glue, something toxic, something not new which all would be gifted to us by our well-meaning auntie Viv and very often through own our own naivety and foolishness we would attempt to use these things instead of putting them straight in the bin so that no one could be hurt or killed. Over the next few years Cheryl and I shared a house together as we went shambling from one disaster to the next, but that is another story!

For now my mind was back on Dover beach and as mum's rear end greeted the soft canvas of the chair (or bastard bloody cow son chair as she whimsically referred to it) the chair offered no resistance and mum kept on travelling through the canvas arse first and was only met by resistance when her rear end connected with the harsh sand below as bastard chair's frame then completed its manoeuvre collapsing in around mum imprisoning her completely while simultaneously forcing her arms up to her head in a "I surrender" motif, tragically though held in each of her hands were two Mr Whippy style ice creams that would now never be eaten as they were forced onto each side of her head like a pair of devil horns as she crash landed without grace. This by comparison made her roller booted tumble over the bonnet of a parked Datsun Cherry look serious and dignified by comparison.

Memories like these, the ones that make you laugh out loud and cry at the same time have a habit of lying dormant in the vista of the mind until the strangest of times or the most unlikely reminder frees them. I smiled at thought of the rescue party trying to free mum from the deck chair, all I remember was that there was speedos all around her and a new audio library of swear words that were recorded and added to the "must use those at school later bank" that much I remember and without warning another childhood memory entered my mind that I instantly fell upon, the magical mystery tour had come to take me away, although now long abandoned with a tragic history all of its own I had the next stop of our unplanned journey was marked in my mind and after a little button mashing on my trusty sat-nav screen we made our way to the car, we were headed down the coast to Dungeness.

Chapter Six: Perfick

Our time in Kent was coming to an end and we decided to make the most of our last day before our road trip took us to uncharted territories. we had stayed the night in Dungeness nature reserve with the nearby Denge Island a stone throw from our hotel we decided and early morning trek out to see the outstanding engineering achievement which is now known as the sound mirrors (thankfully now a protected and listed monument). The sound mirrors are the genius invention of William Sansome Tucker, the mirrors a precursor to radar, created and positioned in a foreboding flooded quarry, the water deathly deep and unwelcoming they are a sight to behold, the very sight of them ignited my interest in urban exploring and my curiosity for military installations and nuclear bunkers. Michaela and I still avidly visit these marvels whenever we get the time. I don't pretend to understand our subterranean history fully, but I'm still fascinated by it and I will happily listen for hours to anyone that can enlighten me on the subject.

The Mirrors were designed to pick up the rumbling sounds of enemy aircraft coming in from the channel were the first early warning system of their kind giving the RAF time to scramble planes from as far away as Biggin Hill to repel the enemy aircraft, the mirrors were large and cumbersome and were an effort to build but in the absence of any alternative they were erected across strategic locations in the UK, soon the invention of Radar followed and the sound mirrors were obsolete almost as soon as they were finished, many left abandoned to be discovered many years later by enthusiasts determined to secure their place in our history, thankfully now many still remain due to the hard work and efforts of the army of volunteers that look after them, preserve them and open them up for us all to enjoy and understand.

After the long walk around the Mirrors we had not only seen the mirrors we drove a short distance along coast through the reserve stopping occasionally to take photographs of the fishing boats and the dunes, just before lunch we boarded the Romney, Hythe and Dymchurch railway taking us to Dymchurch for fish and chips which we ate on the beach in the beautiful summer sun, popping into the various shops as we made our way along to see the Dymchurch Martello tower. Stopping at a little chic hippie boutique Michaela spotted a beautiful white and purple summer dress, looking stunning she changed into it ditching her more practical clothes from our hike earlier, feeling the warmth on her shoulders she smiled happily as we tucked into a post lunch ice cream.

We soon arrived at the imaginatively named tower twenty-four; it formed a part of a much larger redoubt complex. The tower itself was opened in 1969 for the public to enjoy, it is a beautiful building preserved by the national trust their experts sensitively and diligently recreating and restoring the interior perfectly. Sitting just behind the sea wall the tower was largely being ignored by the throngs of people passing it on their way to the sandy beach and the little funfair. It was all ours for a brief and joyful half hour. The redoubt is still privately owned and is opened occasionally by its owner (the ministry of defence). The Redoubt is left on my bucket list of things to do as it will I'm sure provide a fascinating look into our Napoleonic wartime history.

We continued our journey on the little railway up to Romney Marsh to see the model railway exhibition which was beautifully crafted and was worthy of Rod Stewart 9perhaps one off the most famous model railway enthusiast) it depicted the history of the railway itself. We spent a lazy hour with a cake and a bottle of drink each in the open air of the platform watching the comings and goings of people and the arrivals and departures of the little trains, I was enthralled by the faces of the little children that looked on in wonder as these tiny marvels of engineering rattled past them, the children's squeals of delight was as refreshing as our drinks and just as welcome. Our cakes eaten and drinks consumed we wandered through the small, well thought out and informative railway museum.

The Railway itself was built as a private enterprise by John Edwards Presgrave Howey and Count Louis Zbrowski two millionaire racing car drivers that felt the need for some steam powered speed; tragically Louis was killed in a motor race in 1937 before he could experience the joy of his creation. John pressed on and had the railway finally finished in 1927 and it was used with enthusiasm and joy until the outbreak of world war Two. The army took control of the railway in 1940 it was duly armed and used for a mixture of purposes often carrying vital supplies to soldiers stationed along the coast as well as carrying working anti-aircraft guns that could easily be manoeuvred into place as needed at very short notice, fast moving and able to operate in complete darkness it proved itself to be a very able and efficient ally.

The railway survived all attempts on it and it was opened again for pleasure by Laurel and Hardy in 1947, they visited the railway as part of their famous UK tour, Michaela and I had the privilege of seeing the Laurel and Hardy trains in action as the railway trust dedicated two of the engines in their honour. The railway has been run for the pleasure of generations ever since and remains one of the best examples of its kind in the world.

The train bought us back into Dungeness we was delighted to find with just enough time to see it's lighthouse, as we prepared to burn off the copious amounts of food we had consumed throughout the day we started our clamber up the one hundred and forty steps to the top. We was rewarded by the most stunning views across the

English channel and across the nature reserve itself, Michaela took her camera out and happily used its functions that were far beyond my capabilities, she changed lenses and settings with confidence and ease, capturing the all-encompassing views she turned her attention to the inner workings of the lighthouse which were perfectly preserved. Michaela it was transpiring was adept at urban photography, capturing each intricate cog or inner working perfectly making the ordinary into art. Although decommissioned in the late 1960's the internal workings are all still there to be seen and appreciated and as Michaela busily put her camera to use I read the history of the lighthouse, it was now sadly redundant as the build-up of shingle on the coast had made its position irrelevant and a newer automated lighthouse now stood proudly in place.

I made a note to myself that we should stop on our way to Lands' End to see Portland Bill Light house on the Isle of Portland on the coast of Dorset giving me a nice break in the drive while providing us the perfect diversion. I remembered that my sister Cheryl had for her school trip in the mid-eighties stayed in Dorset and with my memory jogged and after a little searching we had decided that we would head to Dorset and spend a couple of nights there, with our plans changing I rang Cheryl and to my delight she remembered some of the places she had visited, so along with Portland Bill and the nearby fort. We decided that we had time also to see Corfe Castle and take in the towns of Weymouth and Poole. I was delighted to find that the hotel that was the childhood home of my Hero Tony Hancock had a free room for the next two nights and with accommodation in Lands' End not yet sorted things had aligned perfectly. With the promise of the next few day's adventures in the air we made our way back to the car, still amazed by the free parking sign we climbed in to the car, I was about to sleep under the same roof that comedy legend once called home, little did I know that we would also be sleeping in a haunted house as the secrets of the hotel's history would reveal.

The nature reserve with its light house dunes and channel views along with the Romney and Hythe Railway is one of the many gifts that Kent has offer, the garden of England was the backbone of two world war operations for both the Navy and the Airforce it is steeped in History both military and domestic, It is my home county and I'm very proud of it. It has castles dating back thousands of years along with hundreds upon hundreds of country homes and important properties to visit all boasting their own stories and ghosts. The coastline is as stunning as its open spaces and forts. It boasts two of the finest zoological parks in the country. The Aspinall Trust has worked tirelessly to promote the wellbeing and growth of many endangered species with its world-famous breeding and release programs. As One of Kent's most famous Son's would attest "its perfick".

We headed west and was soon on the M23, a packed day behind us my mind soon turned to the road trip ahead, I was excited to be returning to the West Country a place that I had visited often in my teenage years with my good friend Christian, We used to head to the west country for a few weeks away during the summer with his mum, we was fifteen, horny and seriously lacking in the skills to do anything about it. The thought of Fistral beach and a summer of adventures kept us going as we worked on any odd jobs that came our way in the desperate bid to earn money for much illegal beer.

Chapter Six: baked potatoes, the road and Rod

The long and winding road, in supposition leads to the door of your loved one. Eventually given time it would lead us west, back to one of the happiest times in my childhood. We would soon be headed to Llangollen which was the first place at the grand age of eleven that I had my first real holiday all alone with 33 of my classmates and the other half of the school. I revelled at the idea.

In my final summer at Tubbenden Junior School we that are my gang and me (Lee, Jason, Dan, Richard and Michael) were to be let loose for a glorious week of outbound adventure. It is often said you never have friends like the ones you had growing up and I was excited at the prospect that we off to the beautiful Shropshire countryside and the Welsh borders. Boreatton Park, Telford was to be our home for the week, I didn't know it at the time, but these guys were some of the greatest friends I ever had. I'm honoured to say that even now almost Forty years after us first meeting in Mrs Walker's reception class I still have every single one of them in my phone. I've met many other friends along the way, but these guys join Danny and Ben with a few others Andy, Justin and Christian to be true friends that have defined my life. I love them all.

It was one of those summers that were long and hot. The smell of opportunity for all of Thatcher's children hung in the air. The summer signalled in many ways the end of my childhood, an uncomfortable thought hung in the air for us, The unspoken menace that at the end of this holiday and in the following last short weeks of term we would all go our own ways as secondary school beckoned for us and the uneasy transition into adulthood would weave its unstoppable course. Some of my most abiding memories are from this period in my life, all happy and all optimistic.

My head full of memories and excited at the prospect of a few days nostalgia we headed out of Dover and after a short while we were on our way up the M20 London bound. I reflected on the smiling faces in those blurry holiday pictures and lamented on the faces that I no longer knew and wondered what path life had taken them on, hoping that the joy in those pictures had carried on for friends I no longer knew, sadly not everyone are still with us and the march of time has been kinder to some more than others but excited by my memories I couldn't wait to show Michaela the sights and sounds of my adventures I had with the gang more than thirty years earlier, not exactly an Atlantic crossing but just as important and dear to me.

I was shaken from my reverie by some arseholed trucker from Denmark blowing his horn and temper in equal measure having not enjoyed being cut up, brake checked and finger fucked by a rather doubtful looking 2CV (you know the car, yellow bastard that looks like a Fiat 500 has fucked a pram) it was being driven by what I can only describe as the love child of Adolf Hitler and Boy George. The hair on this guy was absolutely stunning!

If the adage that speed kills is correct, I'd too buy a Citroen 2CV and look smug and pious with the comfort that I too would live forever with a humble 2CV, the boast of nought to sixty in a fortnight ensuring my sweet arse would never be a risk of sliding fast into the grave sideways screaming fuck me! What a ride! With a CV, I wondered if this information was ever stated in the sales brochure, whether some clever marketing panel with lust for everything naff decided to just claim that the feat could be achieved "eventually" thus avoiding any legal trouble later, or if they though to add the tagline "it goes" My mind flitted to thoughts of men in wigs also not being troubled by wind resistance of a 2CV pulling away under harsh acceleration, I considered for a moment if there was another advertising angle that Citroen had missed? Should I tell them I thought I was certain I had hit gold just as the trucker decided today was the day I was to die as he swerved his truck towards my car. I hit the brakes while inviting him to go forth and be fruitful (but not in those words).I decided then after all with all things considered that a 2CV isn't that bad and would be worth having just to point under the wheels of Denmark's finest to stop his decent into madness. Soon Mad Max was in my rear-view mirror I felt sorry for him, the poor thing was obviously miles from home and in need of some sexual relief.

The day for us was already long, we had slept badly the previous evening in a local Stalag where, in the room next to us the sweet sound of a Baboon making love to a Walrus as an elephant played a bassoon or Tuba in accompaniment but not in time with, the said lovemaking, soon Michaela was drifting in and out of sleep her face beautiful she seemed relaxed. For company I switched on the Audi's complex and often frustrating sound system and after some fiddling and mild swearing the Sound of Rod Stewart filled the car.

Rod Stewart was an absolute favourite of my mum and my Uncle Paul modelled himself on Rod a bit, even though he never cared to admit the fact, it was Paul's extensive and somewhat envied vinyl collection that boasted the greatest Rod Stewart albums, Mum caught the bug for him and his ballads and I as a 10 year old soon was hooked, the bug, it seemed, was hereditary. I have great memories of my mum playing Atlantic crossing and never a dull moment at full volume during the daytime as she went about her housework, the unique style of the riffs competing and failing to score against Rod's powerful voice. A competition that is sheer folly to attempt. Rod Stewart provided the soundtrack to our life and in those days, he always wore it well.

Rod Stewart doesn't so much sing a ballad; he weeps into the microphone and takes you with him through a myriad of emotion. You don't hear Rod Stewart songs, you feel them. The gift he has is remarkable as he performs with such ease, emotion flowing through every bar, an artist of his generation and a genius storyteller he weaves silk. I thought as a kid that he could walk on water and shit Ice cream, a talent and ability that has never diminished and is simply unrivalled, he was the natural and only choice to sing a final farewell song to my Mum at her funeral, for many years after and still now I can't get to the end of Kiss her for me without shedding tears. Beautiful in every way he bought a few minutes of calm composure for me to mum's goodbye and was without doubt the catalyst for my decision to run away.

I have strict instructions that when it's my time to go I will be sent on my way to farewell, one of my most cherished and favourite Rod Stewart tracks, I once played farewell to my sister Cheryl and told her it was to be my goodbye song and within seconds of Rod filling the airwaves Cheryl was in tears. I'm also going to hire an actor to try and jump in the hole with me when its time but I'm not sure if that would be one step beyond. I also like the idea of a tabernacle band following my coffin down the street as the bastards all try to keep me on their shoulders as their knees bow under my weight. Failing that I'd be quite happy to be popped in a wheelie bin or shot out of a cannon.

Rod was there for me in the beginning as he will be at the end, I had my first shot of Brandy accompanied by unplugged and seated and had my first break up to have a told you lately. Most people, born on this planet will have someone or something that follows them throughout their life, my sister Cheryl has James Dean, Donna has Robbie Williams and Beccy, well she is the exception as she has a very unhealthy interest in the alleged comedian Jason Manford, she loves him dearly in her own wonderful and unique way. I'm not sure if I could stand having him as a brother-in law especially if he decides to send me one of his ropey chat up porno texts.

My secondary school friend Christian was different in many ways, sensitive and emotionally clever and strong he was a world championship dancer as a youth and is now one of the most respected and sought after dance teachers in the world living in Hong Kong and travelling all over the world, He as a teenager knew what he liked and while the world around him consisted of Buffalo Stance and dub be good to me he was all about the mood music, often teased (along with myself) for being a bit poofy although ironically by the age of 14 he had shagged more girls than most of the bullies ever will. I would even go so far as to bet that even now they aren't touching the numbers that he hit before he turned 16, that aside Chris was one of the few people that I found a kindred spirit in, Kind, loyal and remarkably always his own person he had a quiet strength and the serenity to walk away from conflict, knowing he had nothing to prove, like me he was an absolute sucker for Rod's unplugged and seated album and in the years that followed we would crack open a bottle of whatever drink was fashionable (not free!) and have ourselves a party Chris, Me and Rod with the former getting more and more drunk with each repeated play we would listen, lament and plot into the small hours.

Chris has been a big part of my life for more than thirty years and although I don't see him anywhere near as much as I would like our love of Rod and music is the bond that binds us and wherever he is in the world he always lets me know he has had a safe journey (he has just touched down in Australia). Chris was there when I first moved out of home and kept me company through some difficult times, Rod has followed us through life, along with Chinese takeaway, women and through many, but nowhere enough bottles of Scotch. We had great holidays in our mid-teens in the West Country, but I won't spoil that bit here suffice to say the highlights are he strokes a dead sheep and falls in a river.

A lot like Chris but in a very different way Mum's gift to me was her love of music, when the music played it normally meant that things were good, the bills were paid for another month and there was food in the fridge and if we were lucky there would be a bottle of cola resting there too as she completed the Friday big shop. I can remember one time that sticks in my memory my sister Cheryl had gone to a birthday dinner with one of her obviously more affluent friends to a place that filled me with wonder called Beefeater, now it's a well know stable that is often overlooked and ignored by the masses, often mistook as a brand of gin now, but back then it was exciting and different especially to someone like me who had only eaten food not cooked at home out of newspaper!

In Cheryl's absence mum made one of my favourites the humble jacket potato, after what seemed like an eternity or at least a month in the oven the potatoes were ready, I asked mum if she thought there was a restaurant somewhere called potatoeaters, never to see me left out as we sat eating our fayre mum decided that we should be called the potatoeaters and if there wasn't a restaurant as such then there should be and it would be the best place on earth, I knew she felt bad for me being left behind as she let me have around 3 packets of butter with my Potato. A simple kindness and a simple conversation that has endeared itself with me, looking back I'm not sure if this memory has stayed with me for so long because I rarely had my mum all to myself and this time just a simple meal, me and my mum together talking about nothing but bonding so indelibly. I remember her laughing as she told me about the time I got jealous of Danny's smart wedding outfit as he was to be a page boy at his sister's wedding and because I didn't have a new suit I exacted my malevolent revenge by tipping a shovel full of dirt all over him, he moved so quick after the shovelling I had no time to smear him with the dog shit. The only satisfaction I had that day was our neighbour Vic got obscenely drunk at the after party and passed out and puked on Danny with a stunning degree of gusto.

When the weather is bad and Michaela and I have jacket potatoes I think of mum (silly I know) and think about her, her easy way, her kind words and her gentle smile. As I sit writing in my office at home in the middle of the harsh Somerset winter tears roll still and my pain and loss is less abated. On the day that would have been my beautiful mum's 63rd birthday as if by magic the play list on my computer filled the room with you'll always be a part of me and like an old raincoat that never lets you down Rod Stewart. I like to think its mum's way of letting me know she knows.

Life in the late seventies and early eighties could be tough. Bills had to be paid and the big utility companies didn't have the social awareness they have now. Things financially were very tough for us, looking back as an adult making an OK living, I can't comprehend how my mum coped and kept things together, but she did, and we had a happy home life with fantastic Christmases surrounded by family. Music wasn't a huge part of family life, but it had the ability to gel us together. We would often pile into whatever hideous monster of a car my mum had at the time, crank on the stereo and in some cases mono and rock out to our favourite tunes, we once had an old allegro or some other lump and I remember a trip we took in it to see my auntie Viv we were being conscripted into a holiday with her and just a few days before the poor old allegro's mono finally did the decent thing and died unperturbed we got some batteries and took Cheryl's cassette player from her bedroom with us, we listened to Beautiful South nearly all the way to Dover carefree happy times that don't seem possible now. The journey in the car used to be part of the adventure, part of the excitement of a day out now you see car loads of people wearing headphones and tanning themselves in the radiating glow of their mobile phones. Not much chance of a sing along!

It's funny all the things you think about when you are driving it can be a very cathartic exercise and useful way to spend time, it's part of the reason I love driving and I thoroughly enjoy being with my thoughts as villages, hills and fields roll past me, more so now than back then as I can think about mum and laugh about something silly she said or did which to my relief is something I couldn't do back then. The road ahead of us was clear, the evening sun lay high in the sky, and the song Convoy by C.W McCall drifted through the speakers sparking memories of another institution from my childhood.

Before Beccy and Donna came along, Cheryl and I would for a rare treat be taken by mum when she had enough petrol for a drive. We would pile into the car and be taken for a short spin around the local lanes down through the Darrent valley, from the back seat of the car we watched the world go by, looking out of the back window we would spook ourselves looking into the darkness, winding each other up that we were being chased by some beast or other. We enjoyed these moments on the road, getting out of the overcrowded house to spend a little while with mum. A simple pleasure that cost next to nothing and meant the world and probably gave me my passion for driving.

On occasion we would visit our cousins in Farningham and on the drive back as we sprinted in our little Austin 1300 the headlights would hit the trees that lined the narrow lanes forming ghastly witch like shadows across the back seat exhilarating and frightening us in equal measure. As we neared home we was faced with a fork in the road, it led to the same place but spilt to a higher and lower road, as we approached mum would shout "higher or lower", if we was feeling brave we would both shout "higher" which would take a past what was rumoured to be the local haunted house, after a quick scream we would be past and back onto the main road.

The world to us back then seemed much smaller, trips to the coast that was a little over an hour in reality seemed like an eternity as we travelled the A roads winding our way through Kent, long before the motorway network was created. The short hop by car from our cousin's house in nearby Farningham was one of the many highlights of day spent with them and it was just as much part of our excitement and the days adventure.

It was always great fun visiting Georgie and Matthew and our auntie Chris was one of the most awesome people you could ever meet, she was a powerhouse of artistic talent and energy. A nurse by calling and a mum by nature. She always kept us entertained whether it was fishing in the local stream down in the Darenth valley or making arts and crafts she was up for it all.

We would all be sat down without fail mid-afternoon to eat a meal of beans, spam and chips which would set the scene for much messing about and giggling often leading to one or several of us being sent into another room to calm down, it was all part of the silly ritual and the fun. We would play endless games of swing ball and attempt unsuccessfully to play board games that would end up as they do in a terrific fight that would be as enjoyable as the game itself.

There were stand out times when we the girls would make rose petal perfume and us boys would attempt to produce itching powder, that to be honest never worked but did smell much better than the perfume. In all fairness we never really achieved a power like substance it was more a heap of wet shit in a bag but never the less We would spend the day smearing this unqualified shit over each other and spend the next three hours asking each other if we was itching yet. It was no surprise when Matthew went on to become a professor of science enjoying much success in his field, I really must remember to ask him if he ever managed to create itching power.

One day Georgie had had an argument with Chris over what I can't now remember, she had taken herself off down to the garages, which was exactly what it said on the tin, a row of garages separated in two by a very narrow gap into which Georgie had run into and was now hiding out in, I can remember the fruitless attempts to retrieve her. In the fullness of time I can't remember how long she stayed there but I recall admiring her staying power to my young mind she stayed there so long she missed her post dinner malt loaf.

At the end of a long day we would all pile back into mum's old car and make the journey home tired and happy. Sadly, we lost Chris far too soon, she is forever young in our hearts and minds and is an inspiration to us all, her naughty humour and impish personality was a joy. I remember her fondly and imagine her now sat with mum enjoying a joke, laughing her unmistakable laugh a broad smile lighting the room.

Chapter Seven: Westbound and down

The greatest thing about a road trip is the film, or at least a road movie Smokey and the Bandit, Cannon ball run, and Convoy all stick in my mind. The gravitas of the great Kris Kristofferson in stark contrast to Burt Reynold's flawed hero the Bandit. Both incredible actors and absolute heroes of mine. Burt Reynolds was always a joy to watch and although he himself regretted some of his choices never fails to make me smile. The Cannonball Run and The Bandit films are my go to feel good films, feeling sick Smokey and the Bandit would go on the screen as the duvet simultaneously sung me to sleep, the number of the emergency services clutched tightly in my fist as bravely battled man flu. I loved the complex relationships that played out in the Smokey films, you had the young dynamic Bandit the quintessential broke but upbeat hero taking his chances where he can contrasting the brilliant Jackie Gleason as the jaded sheriff who stumbled just short of greatness, consumed by the prospect of what never. Always just falling short and missing the prize throughout the film as one disaster after another mirroring his life is played out to my absolute delight. The blossoming real life romance between sally Field and Burt Reynolds is only too obvious and makes a perfect partnership as the on screen chemistry between them is palpable as Burt's vulnerability as a person and an actor is revealed every time he looks at Sally Field, I was sure he was seeing the person not her character.

Burt Reynolds embraced his southern routes and did all he could to promote talent in the south, whether it was insisting his films be shot there giving a precious boon to local economies or championing new southern talent. He donated his time to teach younger actors and gave them opportunities on his films, He loved his craft and was clever beyond the credit of most, he loved hard and worked hard, He should in my opinion and that of many have won an Oscar for Deliverance, but it wasn't to be. I admire Burt because he walked his own path, choosing the southern recording styles of Jerry Reed to soundtrack his films along with a host of other southern stars when the trend was definitely heading in a different direction. He drew upon the wonderful Hal Needham as a director he was loyal to his friends, giving opportunity to his stuntman colleagues, he was honest in an industry that often wasn't often putting the interests of others above his own.

For anyone that has dismissed these films as tosh, give them a go they are genuinely funny and have the feel-good factor baked right in. Enough time has passed and Burt's impact on the film industry is justified, he was the biggest box office star of the eighties, his passion for acting was with him throughout his life, he founded an acting school that charged no fees and he helped local communities and many charities, never talking about his commitments to others he proved to be truly altruistic with his distinct lack of self-promotion.

The Cannonball run has it all, Burt, Dom De Louise, the rat pack and some incredible cars. The action and comedy are blended beautifully, Roger Moore parodies himself as a wannabe James Bond and Farrah Fawcett is perfect as she drives Mr Foyt wild with desire. There are so many things to love about this film, it was one that I could always watch with my mum and she would laugh with me at it, everyone was invited along for the ride. The storyline is irrelevant it is like a family reunion at Christmas the film welcomes you in and asks nothing from you, it has feuding brothers, mad uncles and the occasional superhero, oh and Jackie Chan! My teenage years were spent watching these films with my friends along with the any which way and Blues Brothers films they were always our go to movies, as I got older Burt and Clint Eastwood were joined by Charles Bronson, Bill Murray and Steve Martin as firm favourites joined by the talented Michael Caine and Richard E Grant as my experience of film grew.

I have been passionate about film for as long as I can remember, many happy hours I would spend watching, Ealing comedies, the Marx Brothers, Laurel and Hardy along with Carry on films and any number of classic British comedies ranging from St Trinians to School for scoundrels. I loved watching Sid James, Will Hay, Terry Thomas, Ian Carmichael and the talented stars of 50's and 60's comedy. Nothing was lost on me I devoured films rapaciously.

I was later influenced by My uncle Paul, picking up his love for Monty Python, Marty Feldman, Mel Brooks and the wonderful and talented Gene Wilder, I became quite the film buff soaking up classics from It's a mad mad world to Harold and Maude with the great Ruth Gordon while taking in Joe's Orton's masterpieces Loot and Entertaining Mr Sloane as I went. One film I was introduced to by Christian was the night before we were due to travel to Par in Cornwall, after some hard work cutting grass and washing cars, we sat ready to go full of excitement. Christian was staying at our house for the evening and his mum was due to pick us up in the morning, armed with a view VHS films coerced out of his mum from the rental shop. Chris opting for volume of films to see us through had found some great films from the comedy section, in the now long forgotten pile of films was a stand out for me, it introduced me to Steve Martin and ignited my love for him that has still not abated.

If ever I am put in the position of revealing my favourite film of all time I would be hard pushed but I am still in love with the British hit film Withnail and I as I was the day I first saw it, each time I watch it I am spellbound by Richard E Grant, I marvel at him, his presence on screen is unrivalled, the scene when I (Marwood) is offered an acting job and is going to leave Withnail played by Richard E Grant, Richard tells him "well done" in one line he delivers a masterclass of acting, honest poignant and true. It is almost painful for me to choose my favourite, but I can watch Withnail over and over again seeing something new each time, my other great favourite in contrast is Harry brown played by the majestic Michael Caine.

Sir Michael is at his best as he plays the seminal protagonist Harry Brown, a widower scared by life and the violence he encounters on his estate is driven to extremes by the loss of his best friend. Beautifully acted I soak up the performances, its gritty and entertaining. I adore the Italian job, sleuth and Alfie equally, but I think its Sir Michael's understated performance in this film combined with subject matter that does it for me, I recommend it enormously. I love to watch it back to back with Clint Eastwood's Gran Torino when I feel in the mood to set the world right.

I find it interesting that many of my favourite films no matter what the genre, Romance, comedy or my beloved road movies all have a shared theme, they all explore human relationships, in their own way they peered into the cracks of humanity looking at how complex we are as humans, whether it's a frustrated backwater Sheriff rolling the dice one more time in a final bid for glory and that elusive thrill of success or two friends locked in a co-dependent relationship set on the road destruction, even going on holiday by mistake.

Complex issues can be addressed in different ways, yes we can look too far into things and become a bit whiney maybe even a little wanky, I remember my English teacher and her constant obsession with the hidden meaning of things, constantly searching for a hidden meaning or a subtext that simply wasn't there she would put the question to us as we boiled to death in her windowless classroom "but what does the author really mean? What is the significance of the boy looking into the mirror? What does this tell us about the selective evolution of man?" it became tedious, I wanted to scream at her "it's fucking Adrian Mole Miss, He is looking in the mirror to count his spots, spots are funny now move on you dappy bastard" but alas I never did. We got through English just about.

We loved it really our teacher Miss Antrobus was a strange lady forever throwing us curve balls... She would often sit in her chair in various states of alcohol fuelled stupor ranging from regretful hangover to whimsical shitface (which we loved) she would make up things off the top of her head allowing us all to get away with murder. Even the biggest swots in the class would join us in Swearing blind she never set us homework the previous lesson knowing she wouldn't argue. After one of her "happy days" We could have told her she had taken a shit in Maria Perkin's tuba and she would have believed us. She was dressed always in grey from her grey hair down to her grey tights, there was never a hint of colour about her until you reached her shoes, in perfect contrast they were a deep red colour with a slight sparkle to them. With her shoes it was like looking at a black and white picture of Minnie Mouse where the only the shoes had been colourised.

Miss Antrobus had a mild obsession with keeping everyone out of the building at lunch time and a massive addiction to fags that she smoked with gusto wherever and whenever she could, not a lesson went by where one essay or another wasn't returned to us with a fag burn in it, often disappearing to run a non-existent errand returning to the class stinking of fags whilst sporting a slightly satisfied look about the eyes. We would pray the night before our English lesson if we had done a particularly bad job on a piece of work that ours would be the one that she burned to cinders at home while falling asleep as she marked it with a fag in her hand a bottle of plonk to her side, as she lamented the day that house had fell on top of her sister, at least I guess she inherited the shoes.

To ease her boredom and to feed her distain for children, she policed the doors into the school building with a crack heavily trained commando unit, her bastion of monkeys ensured her regime was far reaching and brutal, "oh is it raining? Fuck off and get wet then", "you haven't got a coat? Well your dad should have tried harder at school then you dolt" she was a hard nut to crack but blisteringly funny with it, being told off by Miss Antrobus was like being told to fuck off by Rik Mayall or Billy Connolly, it was absolutely awesome.

It's funny the things your mind turns to when you have only the open road in front of you, The day had been long and hard and I was glad of the break in our journey, we had finished the last stretch of our journey, eventually arriving at the Hotel Celebrity. I carried the bags out of the car as Michaela went ahead to check us in, I was immediately drawn to the blue plaque that sat next to the front door professing proudly that this was indeed the site of Tony Hancock's childhood home. Standing just next to it was a red phone box inside which there was a short but informative card telling the reader that the hotel in its heyday was used by many stars of the day and the press wouldn't be above paying the hotel staff to listen in to the phone calls made from the rooms within the hotel soaking up as much scandal as they could, realising this the owners not wanting to have his guests privacy and affairs compromised arranged for the phone box to be installed operated directly by the GPO it was safe place for any star or starlet to plan and plot to their hearts content. Without taking a footstep inside I was head over heels in love with the place.

To my delight each room had a celebrity theme, keen to stay in the Hancock themed room I was crestfallen when I was told by a rather embarrassed check in manager the hotel and former home of Tony Hancock indeed had no Hancock themed room. I could see the stress that years of explaining to guests this fact on a daily if not hourly basis had taken, with quivering lips and pulsing vein in his forehead he summoned up the strength to go through the whole thing again. Sensing his pain, I quickly interjected that it was fine and accepted the keys to the David Bowie room.

We unpacked our things and settled into our room, I was grateful to sink into a long hot bath washing away the long drive, I thought about what lay ahead over the next few days, I was excited to explore this part of the world, Old Harry's rock and Corf Castle awaited us the following day and as feelings of incredible tiredness overtook me I was soon laying in the big hotel bed, drifting into a fitful sleep.

Chapter Eight: Old Harry and the snooper

Old Harry's Rock, forms part of the beautiful Jurassic coast, nestled at the southernmost tip at Handfast Point, it is a stunning part of the coastline, it isn't too dissimilar from the Seven Sisters coast in East Sussex. Old Harry, as legend would have it has a few origins. My favourite is that of the Devil being called Harry (He seemed more like an Ernest or a Cecil to me) who fell asleep under the rocks his rumbling disquiet leading to the cliffs slowly but surely fall away into the sea. The legend is somewhat confused as others believed that the rocks adopted their name from the infamous pirate Harry Paye who was known as the devil of the sea who hid with his gang among the rocks waiting for seafaring vessels to plunder under the cover of darkness. Either way Old Harry is held in the affections of the locals and is guarded by them jealously.

We arrived at the picnic site just in time for lunch, met by perfect blue skies and coastal views, as we sat eating our sandwiches, scotch eggs and sausage rolls two elderly ladies passed us by in deep conversation. I am fascinated by the tail end of conversations, not that I eaves drop intentionally but occasions when an erroneous mobile phone is left on a desk or table that you are sitting at your eyes are inadvertently drawn to its devil like glow as you try to resist the secrets etched on the screen you can't help but see it, as much as you try not to be that person, you know the one that gets a bit wet when you hear a bit of gossip, unless you stick your fingers in your ears and scream you will overhear things no matter how hard you try not to,

I call it adventures in inadvertent snooping as that seems about right. Peeping however is always a definite no-no and I will run like hell if I hear sex noises, thankfully though the risks of that diminish as I get older and my friends become more sensible and less restricted in the places they can "do it", thankfully not having to make do with a quick jump in a corner or a few moments hidden under a duvet while your mates are trying to watch Robocop.

My favourite two inadvertent snooping adventures couldn't be more different, the first happened while I was desperately trying to resist the temptation to plug myself into the national grid whilst avoiding, unsuccessfully I might add the opportunity to swell the coffers of a well know Swedish led mafia outlet know not for pushing drugs to kids but meatballs and high storage capacity furniture durables to adults. I was stood contemplating throwing myself from the mezzanine level down to the market place below, as I pondered where I had gone wrong a couple walked by engaged in vigorous conversation, brilliantly the young lady wore a T-shirt emblazoned with Sexy written across the front, the young man with whom she was caught mid flow with wore a suitably matching shirt with Debateable written on it, the joke I was sure was lost on his partner. While I stood, I prayed that a Billy bookcase would strike me on the head sparing me by the will of a gracious the god the misery of the marketplace where I could choose from three thousand different designs of forks.

As the couple who were by now fast becoming my favourite people in this place idled past me, I caught the tail end of the girl's sentence "and if I don't use it, I can keep it in my arse until I'm ready". I hadn't laughed as much since someone had used one of the changing rooms in our local branch of Peacocks as a toilet, having picked number two from a list of numbers ranging from one to two, I remembered the pure horror of the situation, you could read the face of every single member of staff, there was only one question on their minds and it was palpable, who the fuck was going to clean that!

Never more than at that stage did I want to know the whole story of sexy and debatable, alas though as soon as they entered my life they departed it and as I hadn't the luck to have departed this realm by hand of god or otherwise I accepted my fate and succumbed to life as a trolley wanker with all the other poor souls driven into a buying madness after an orgy of meatballs and gravy. I'm convinced to this day that there is a conspiracy where the meatballs are laced with drugs by various government agencies and powerful billionaire investors in order to make you crave meatballs and self-assembly furniture once a fortnight. You can get your thrills elsewhere but if you put them together yourself, they do get them cheaper.

My second adventure in inadvertent snooping was as these two serene and very well to do ladies who passed us by dressed in their summer dresses with their genteel hats perched on their heads, they chatted as only old friends or sisters do, one said about a person unknown "he is a dog fancier you know?" the other lady full of wry wisdom replied back as quick as a flash "yes, I was rather afraid he was" needless to say I choked on my lunch at the multiple connotations of the sentence, again I immediately wanted to know more alas the down side to inadvertent snooping is that you never get to know the full story and rule book is very clear on the matter, you can never continue the snoop when it stops being inadvertent. In my head the man in question I hoped never acted upon his lust for dogs and went on to live a happy full life whereupon he manages to tame his urges avoiding a lengthy prison spell. I suspect however more probably that he went onto a lifetime of misery dragging his loved ones around dog shows while whoring himself around the judge's enclosure in desperate attempts to win the coveted best in show prize in that strange and murky world full of halitosis and regret, I supposed that as long as he didn't try to win the heart and love of the show winner he was best left to it.

The only other issue with overhearing things is when what you hear is so absolutely wrong it becomes comical, you desperately want to correct and educate the noise but you run the risk of exposing the snoop, a few years previously I was travelling on a bus in Bradford, there was what I can only describe as the world's most patient and understanding mother worthy of the greatest mother's day card ever written as sitting next to her was her forty something stay at home single son sporting full membership to the confirmed bachelor club. He was a veritable Henry's cat (he knew everything about nothing and not too much about that) firstly he started to berate his mum about not keeping the tone of her voice to an even tone and volume like they do on the radio making it impossible for him to understand anything she was saying, I suspected at this point that it may not be his mum's uneven tones that was causing the malfunction.

While devouring another crayon with a side order of window his intellect continued to be a source of amazement to me as he cited that Peru was the capital of France, his mum momentarily caught my eye as if to say sorry, I thought at any minute she would either scream at the top of her voice "his father was a nuclear physicist" or jump out of the closed window and expediently alighting the moving bus. Sadly she turned her gaze back to her book "how to commit the perfect murder and get away with it" he chimed in again with what I now consider to be the biggest misunderstanding of the inner workings of the human psyche, Malcom (they are always called Malcom) started to discuss with his poor mum the condition of Asperger's syndrome, a debate that had obviously been the subject of some radio phone in or other, referring to the serious social condition as "arse burgers" labouring under the assumption that it was pronounced arse burgers after a misunderstanding or mishearing the sane voices coming out of his radio, Malcom believing now that it is a slang term for diarrhoea that I his wise and educated opinion could easily be managed through the use of adult and larger sized nappies, This guy was worthy of a position in senior government. I suspect though that he would lack the dishonest disposition required for even the most junior governmental post. I think his mother would have agreed his move to London in a heartbeat.

I have never been able to this day to convince anyone that that this was true and such people are allowed electricity and to wonder around even if it was with their weary mothers. My issue with Malcom was that he was a know it all; blinded by his own sense of self-importance and value he would never listen to anyone with real knowledge or allow them to help him.

As the ladies passed us by we started our walk around the top of the cliff top, the views were truly stunning and the rocks were indeed worthy of the admiration people heaped on them, now long eroded through weather and wave to such an extent that poor Harry's first wife had long crumbled into the sea leaving just Harry and his second wife standing, the erosion so bad that this part of the coast that used to be joined to the Isle of Wight at what is now known as the Needles at Totland on the western most tip of the Island Which is now a tourist attraction in itself that somewhat overshadows the real beauty of the Needles themselves packing in endless sweet shops and make your own sand art stalls. I've always loved coastal and coastline views, although I admit previous to today I have always preferred a countryside view, but my eyes having been opened by the stunning and impressive views from Dungeness lighthouse and the vista of old Harry, I now appreciated the coastline even more, I felt a renewed excitement at the prospect of seeing Lands' End in a few days. Old Harry's Rock is now a world heritage site and the Needles is a now site of special scientific interest. Both unique in their own way I made a note to go back and really appreciate the Needles and learn more about them at my earliest opportunity.

The weather was glorious and August was being very kind to us, Michaela by now was using her camera with increasing enthusiasm she navigated the rocks and its views framing her shots with an almost professional ease, the peninsula location of Old Harry gave us almost full panoramic views contrasting sea, sky against the back drop of the brilliant white rocks. . Michaela's pictures were indeed stunning and were soon filling the memory stick in her camera, the afternoon heat was dry and stifling; we retreated to the soothing cool air of the car's air conditioning as we took the short hop to Corfe Castle.

Corfe Castle is spectacular with the views over the Purbeck Hills perfected over millions of years, the Swanage Railway train steamed into view from Norden through the valley the brilliant white smoke, white as a hospital bedsheet danced in the breeze and floated behind it as it gathered momentum, soon disappearing out of sight. The castle itself was as magnificent as it was imposing; the remaining portions of the castle are very well kept and sympathetically managed. We spent the remainder of the afternoon exploring its history. Built in the tenth centaury by William the Conqueror but much changed in the eleventh and twelfth centuries it stood proud until the seventeenth century when it's pedigree as a royal stronghold was tested as it was held to siege, once it was successfully defended and it was one of the last royal strongholds remaining when it was overrun almost two years later in 1645, sadly like many highly important and high profile buildings of the time it was then slighted on parliaments orders, it sits now as it did then with a beauty all of its own.

My sister Cheryl had told me that when she visited Corfe more than thirty five years earlier her teacher Mr Steere along with the rest of the teachers and volunteers had arranged Cheryl, her classmates and the rest of the school groups to line up at the bottom of the hill the castle and its guard their quarry, the children led by Mr Steere (an excellent teacher and ambassador for the teaching profession in my humble opinion) charged the full run of the hill recreating a little of what the attacking soldiers would have experienced. This type of kinetic teaching delights me, I'm no expert in matters of education but I loved the idea of the children experiencing a little of the exhaustion and endeavour that the invading forces would have experienced. I agree (although he probably doesn't care if I do or not) with Lev Vygotsky that a child's creative thought process is more important than the actual product of creation and that its unimportant what children create as long as they do create. I wish teachers like Mr Steere could still without constraint lead a charge of castle and recite poetry to a cow.

We tracked my sister's well-worn footsteps down the hill and soon my much older body heaved under the stress of a run up the hill, Michaela laughed madly at me as she followed my attack which in the end fell far short of the castle, coming to the sad realisation that I would have died from an arrow up the arse or by being boiled in oil I thought death would be a welcome relief for any poor sod trying to sack this bastard, no wonder it took them two years to beat it.

I enjoyed the stories Cheryl had told about her journey with the school, like me it was the first real break she had on her own. It felt good that I could now tread where she had, Cheryl and I had grown up together for the first six years it was the two of us with Beccy joining us along with Donna shortly after. For a time though it was just us, we were company for each other. Playing and fighting in equal measure like brothers and sisters do we had a lot of fun, I imagined an eleven year old Cheryl running up the him still looking cool with all her cool friends, she was always one of the in crowd and always popular at school, I made a mental note to myself to ask her how she kept her status at cool level as only she could. I found that I needed to talk to her properly, connect with her again, we are still very close but since mum's illness everything had been on auto pilot like we was sleep walking through life, not quite a dream but languid none the less.

The day had been long but rewarding. We had covered a lot of ground and I was looking forward to a nice relaxing meal back at the hotel, Michaela had arranged for us to dine in the Sherlock Holmes restaurant so that we could drink a copious amounts as we wouldn't need to drive anywhere. The late afternoon air was heavy the smell of honeysuckle hung in the air, we sat contentedly on the grass nursing the last dregs of our national trust (special reserve extra awful blend) coffee putting off the inevitable drive back to the hotel. Holding hands, we got our second wind and made our way back to the car as the intense heat of the late afternoon sun gave way to a mellow breeze.

We arrived at our hotel, my earlier thoughts of Cheryl played out in my mind, I hadn't seen my sisters since the funeral and I was dreading the return home, would it still be home? Did I still belong as Mums are the wonderful sweet unseen bond that bind families together, organising and arranging in the background invisible to everyone else they weave the magic of togetherness almost seamlessly, I felt determined not to let her neat stitching unravel or be picked apart, as Michaela busied herself getting ready for dinner I decided to make the first step towards home. After a little searching through bags of cameras, camcorders and untold wires I eventually found my phone in my jacket pocket where I had left it. I switched it on and after some scrolling my sisters voice boomed through the speaker.

Chapter Nine: Gary, Sue and Cheryl too

Cheryl and I grew up in what I think is the best era possible, the internet had not yet cast its shadow over us, and a touchpad was just something we watched on one of the four channels we had on the television. Our Saturdays were spent rushing to the TV to watch our programs before hours and hours of sport would curse our screens once more sending us into the streets to play until Metal Mickey welcomed us back for an evening of game shows and variety. Scooby Doo and Orville the duck was at the top of their game. The Monkees still played out on bank holiday television and Star Wars was still just a reasonably good children's film.

We would walk to our friend's house to see if they wanted to come out to play, any extravagant thoughts of using the phone screwed high up on the wall was merely folly to us. The days were warmer, and the music was better, being four as the eighties started was perfect. Cheryl and I were friends from the off. When I was very small, I followed her round calling her Effie as I couldn't say Cheryl. She was a typical older sister ever so cool as she rubbished my Lenny the Lion programs choosing the much more sophisticated Strawberry Shortcake and Willo the Wisp.

Your brothers and sisters are your first friends, if you are lucky they are your best friend if only for a short time, Cheryl and I in later years were thrown together by circumstance, sharing our first flat we was bound by a common goal which was to survive as teenagers out in the big bad world where you had to pay for things yourself. Before life comes to get you though there is a sweet spot, where there are no bills, no politics and no need to think beyond ensuring you get more of the cola than anyone else. Adulting at least for now was over the horizon and something our parents had to do.

Cheryl was there at the beginning; she has been there my whole life. She is my constant. Mum once told me a story about the time she bought me home from the hospital for the first time, I was shown to Cheryl who remarked "ah, isn't it nice. Now put it in the cupboard". After that I grew on her and according to mum she would make sure each time she was given a biscuit she made sure she had one to give me, happily she would scoot off two biscuits in hand, one and a half for her and a half for me. I didn't mind too much and as I grew, we started to play together, countless Monopoly boards and chess sets were sent into the air in equal measure by Cheryl or myself. During games of Operation countless tens of thousands of pounds would be misappropriated by various parties ending games that would otherwise last for hours through the misuse of various loopholes in rules and outright cheating.

As much as Danny and Ben were my first gang and Jason, Daniel, Lee, Richard and Michael were my gang at school there was always a pause in the fun, those hot summer days when there isn't a friend around as they make their way beaches and theme parks, there are also the days when the darkness won't lift and the rain won't stop when faced with isolation a game with your siblings then doesn't seem so bad. Cheryl and I loved to have a fight; we both won and lost in equal measure.

Cheryl reminded me of a time that on a particularly thundery day, one worthy of Winnie the Pooh, Cheryl at the time had a morbid fear of thunderstorms, the mere suggestion of a black cloud looming innocently on the horizon was enough to send her spiralling like a looney to the nearest toilet with a runny arse. We had our storm drill well and truly perfected, the SAS couldn't have touched our sleek operation. As clouds and thunder started to fill the sky, we would evacuate ourselves to the living room, close the curtains switch on all the lights and crank up the television volume until either we could no longer hear the thunder or ours ears bled. This system served us well, on the odd occasion when the living room was occupied we found retreating to our shared bedroom and stuffing our heads under our pillows would work until mum arrived to tell us not to be so bloody stupid and stop wrecking the beds she had just made. I still don't understand to this day her generation's obsession with immaculately made beds, the use of which was strictly controlled by some inner mum radar system that would scramble any eighties mother to arrive in any given bedroom within three seconds of any hint or suggestion they may be used before the pre-determined bedtime. On one occasion Cheryl was having pleasant hysterics under her pillow as a dark cloud had been spotted over the neighbour's chimney, Mum, radar activated arrived within seconds demanding Cheryl remove herself from the bed "get off the bed I've just made them" (it's strange too that the beds have always just been made) aggrieved Cheryl decried "I don't feel well" which only served to poke the bear "You're not ill, you've just seen a big black cloud over the bloody road now get up and stop whinging, I wouldn't mind so much if only you had decent voices". To this day mum still doesn't know what she meant by that, but we suspect a minor breakdown bought on through bed use related trauma.

The beauty of your siblings is that you all are held captive, you have to forgive each other your childhood sins, and one afternoon Cheryl and I had an intellectual debate regarding the merits of Basil Brush or some other nonsense, in a fit of pique Cheryl took a poster of super group Wham! That I had swapped with Daniel from my gang for a handful of marbles and tore it into pieces denying herself the playful good looks of George Michael and the other one, in simple retaliation and cool silence I smashed her over the head with her toy shopping trolley, which to me seemed a fair and measured response, unfortunately mum didn't agree and we spent the afternoon in our room (but not on the beds).

The best part of being one half of a set of siblings is the games you can play together , the classic made-up ones that everyone would know, your bikes can be red arrow planes, games of schools, doctors and nurses and cowboys and Indians could easily be created without the need for any shop bought toys, anything handy around the house could be pressed into use at a moment's notice. The wardrobe becomes in an instant a prison cell and the bathroom a shop.

Then there are the special sibling type games, the ones that your friends haven't heard of, the made-up games that are born from boredom or shared life experiences. Everything was fair game, at home on a Sunday morning still pyjama clad you could carry around old cookery books pretending they are a set of clandestine instructions ordering you to rob your uncle or knock out next door's cat.

Cheryl and I could be described as a pair of wankers. The games we played were quite out there. We would like most kids of the time make a tent out of an old blanket trussed up with overloaded clothes pegs on the curtain pole with books piled to the sides across any available surface giving the tent its pitch, invariably the books often gave way giving us a sharp smack on the head when we least expected it.

We would play games of twenty all where we played parents who had twenty children each, the game much to mum's disgust would involve our children merrily wrecking the living room of their respective homes, unfortunately this game ultimately banned as every time we played it mum would get irate for some reason that we could never get to the bottom of.

In the summer we would camp out in our tent in the back garden, where a traditional game of mums and dads would take place, soon the mixing of my friends and Cheryl's would result in a hostage situation that invariably would require keen negotiation skills to get out of, Danny soon fed up of sitting in the sweltering tent would complain that he wanted to go and do his stunts (or the pissing around on a bike and falling off show as it became affectionately known). A compromise would soon be reached as we embarked on a new game called "mums and dads and stuntmen". A similar and if not, weirder variation was invented the following day when the game of "bark rubbing and stunt riders" was created. Fearing a theme built on a slight compulsive obsession with stunt riding Cheryl started to drift towards her friends leaving the house of crazy games behind her.

Like Most good things, they come to close at least for a while anyway, your bond as siblings starts to drift, interests change and the age of the self-conscious creeps in and slowly without too much thought you find that your old sparring partner has gone. The house no longer full of forty children and the naughty behaviour books are well and truly put away. Your attempts to leap of the sofa convinced that you could fly if you flap your arms hard enough are no longer shared.

Before you know it your days of watching cartoons with you best friend all too soon gives way to Saturday mornings sat alone, the distant muffled sounds of pop music drifting underneath a firmly closed bedroom door. Part of growing up is growing apart, if you are lucky you will find each other again, united through your teenage years. Cheryl is my much-needed link to the past and part of my future. Her resilience to life astounds me, through each crisis she has taken the mantle, being the backbone of family operations, taking mums neatly stitched and planned blueprints weaving her own unique and humble pattern to it. Her kindness and strength come as no surprise to me, having seen her grow up from being my first friend, to my protector and back to my friend again, losing mum was tough on Cheryl but she wears her grief pride, she carries on the tradition mum set of the proud independent woman. I'm lucky to have her, she will always be a road that leads home.

Chapter Ten: Death and other bonds that bind us

Feeling cooled and refreshed we dined in the Divas restaurant inside the hotel, we had a pretty decent burger and chips each. We decided after dinner that we would have a hunt around the hotel for the ghost and say a quick hello. I decided that the Tony Hancock display case was the best place to start and after much drooling over the small case of Hancock collectables we started our most haunted ghost hunt. I was however starting to suspect that the only place the willies where going to be put up anybody would be in the bridal sweet, feeling distinctly un-molested by the dead we resigned ourselves to an evening with the living. There wasn't even enough paranormal excitement to raise a gnat's erection. I was reminded of the time while in a trance the late ghost whisperer Derek Accorah live on his TV program had repeatedly shouted that Fanny loves Dick over and over again, igniting peels of juvenile laughter from everyone watching.

I once attended an evening with a famous television medium at the Winter Gardens in Folkestone, The show was pleasant enough, the auditorium very much divided, those that were in almost giddy states of rapture pouncing on every detail hoping that the medium, Clive (not his real name) could indeed get faxed and receive messages from the afterlife desperate to be chosen to receive the vital information as to where the old man left the log book to his shitty old car or to find out where great aunt Ethel hid the family jewels. Then there was me and my lot, every time Clive pressed the reset button we slid down into our chairs as he went back online connecting with accuracy of superfast broadband speed to the spirit world without any routing errors, I would have loved the same reliability from my internet provider.

As much as those people sat in hope of a connection I sat with the deep hope that my loved ones in the departed were all out at an all-night scrabble party with Winston Churchill, Ghandi and the cast of Dad's army, desperate not to be chosen and told our loved ones were thinking about us and that they were on the whole pretty pleased with the way they died (don't worry my love he knows you didn't mean to kill him) and that they are quietly enjoying the time spent in the afterlife watching subscription free Netflix whiling away the hours until us remaining poor bastards are ready to give up and join them, suddenly then as soon as they arrive they have to leave possibly because John Le Mesurier had just played oxyphenbutazone on a treble word score.

Suddenly my absolute horror was realised. I was shaken from the bottom of my chair as Clive started chanting my name over and over and within a second a microphone was thrust into my hand and Clive, his eyes meeting mine with a piercing stare began to tell me that I wanted to change my job and start my own business (A pretty safe bet I thought) then something strange happened, Derek connected with my grandad, on my dad's side, he told me that my gamble would pay off and that he was watching over me. He told me that my grandad was willing me on in the afterlife and was my number one fan, pausing for breath his perceptive aura began to fade, I thought the whole experience was astonishing because to the best of my knowledge my grandad was sat at home in Gateshead being a miserable old sod, and above all else remaining very much alive.

Deafened by my bullshit detector I decided that maybe we should all be a little more wary of anyone selling advice. From this point I became and remain sceptical about the actual presence of ghosts and even more so of those selling their abilities to interpret them.

I sat through the whole macabre spectacle willing it to end as people were healed of their aching hearts and limbs, through the medium of mediumship they were finally reunited with loved ones, if not their log books, gems and saving certificates, as we left the auditorium a crowd was gathered around Clive desperate to resist the urge to orgasm as they stood waiting for an autograph suppressing their ever decreasing hope of a quick titting up from the great spiritual leader behind the bins. I thought about the world of spiritualism in general and it all started to seem a bit sinister to me, to be sold through the auspices of private enterprise the notion that one's nearest and dearest can be contacted on demand, to be told they love them and they are at peace (what else are they going to say, piss off, oh he's in constant pain racked in agony day and night he is or that they are knee deep in shit this end) the haunting call that those in heaven are waiting for them to me translated to a slightly more frightening "I'm coming to get you".

The sentiment being that fresh from a call from the afterlife your loved ones are almost willing you to stick your head in the oven so they finally have someone to chill with "come on Flossie", he says "why not kill yourself, you might as well, there is nothing on the telly after all technically your life isn't worth insuring". The whole thing to me seemed wrong and rather exploitative, I remember feeling sad for those that were in so much grief that they would part with virtually anything they possessed to feel that elusive connection and I felt angry at those willing to part them of everything in exchange for their snake oil and promises.

It can be dangerous for those suffering grief to stay in it for too long, it is all too easy to remain in a state of reflection for too long fearing and avoiding the sharp and painful realisation that a your wish or prayer to see or talk to someone again simply won't happen, as much as you would give your last breath to spend a day with them and have that day last forever. The dream of running towards them, picking up speed as you see the beaming smile on their face, your longing to hold and hug them, to laugh with them and really listen to them while hanging on their every word as they tell you how they have been. The grief in us plays with our minds, we weigh up implausible bargains with the universe, trading all of our tomorrows just to spend that one precious day with the one we have lost. It's a destructive emotion and is as dangerous as avoiding the real issue of loss and grief.

Although it is almost impossible to conceive the wait, I knew I must move forward safe in the knowledge that the day will come when I will see mum again, when it is my time. All roads lead home, no matter if you are running away or not. It is important to look forward, to remember the person and keep them close in your heart. Now stood in the middle of our ghost hunt, the healing of time spared me no mercy, loss seared through me, the pain returning with a vengeance of its own, the realisation that there were no more tomorrows for mum, no more Christmases, no birthdays and no quick rings home to tell her I was safe left me numb. I understood I was grieving, but more than that I was wishing my life away, I had wished that I could fast forward my life ten years so the acute pain would subside, I wanted to scream, I knew then that life is the dash between two dates and that mum would want me to make it count. I couldn't fast forward time as much as I wanted to and soon serenity enveloped me and I knew I was ready to carry on, both with life and my ghost hunt which was now almost so farcical I began to laugh as I knew mum would do too, she always relished the ridiculous. Michaela appeared around the corner and pronounced "are you Ok, you look like you've seen a ghost".

The ghostly figure of a little girl who sadly succumbed to tuberculosis is said to wander the hotel in search of comfort, she must have been a good girl because she wasn't seen or heard on our ghost hunt or at all for the duration of our stay .With my deeply sceptical outlook fully engaged all hope of paranormal activity seemed unlikely, although I'm not closed to the idea of ghosts jumping out of wardrobes and scaring people or popping through the occasional wall to say hello but I find rather unlikely that one should be haunting the lift shaft of a Bournemouth hotel, surely there must be a rocking horse knocking about in the attic that she could haunt creating some sort of ritualistic rocking action.

Disappointed by our ghost hunt we decided that a late evening walk would do us good and sans ghost we made our way to the sea front, we approached the pier and made our way along its promenade. The stars hung low in the night sky, the deep blue sea reflected the light of the stars, they shimmered hypnotically as the gentle evening breeze moved the water with a calm ease.

Michaela and I ambled along the sand, the moon provided a still glow, our bellies still heavy from our dinner made us groan, I laboured under the weight of myself, in need of a drink we headed to the old Pier, a beautiful Victorian creation with a beautiful theatre on the end. To my disappointment the pier was closed and without anything else around us eradiating light, we headed towards the town centre, to my surprise the town was a hub of activity, the restaurants and bars sere busy, the town was comfortable and I felt at ease as we settled down in a small bar just off the beaten track, with a drink in hand I sat watching the people walking by, Michaela and I soon started to make up the life stories of the passing people, each story becoming larger and more ridiculous than the last. As the Princess of Tonga passed us carrying a bewildered looking dog in a backpack.

As the early evening cool air gave way to the colder evening breeze which swept in from the sea, it swirled around us as we walked back to our hotel rustling the discarded litter left by the retreating tourists that now sat in the packed hotel bars. The town now almost deserted morphed in appearance the cosmopolitan urbanism gave way to a much more reserved Victorian façade, In the quiet we looked up towards gabled rooftops and sash windows, they looked back at us almost smiling, grateful that we had taken the time to notice. For almost two hundred years they had stood, outlets for food, entertainment and shelter to generations of grateful holiday makers arriving by ever burgeoning steam railway, swelling the coffers of the local community.

The expansion of the railway from London eighty miles away had opened up this beautiful part of the world to the workers of London. Essex to the east and the people of Bristol and beyond to the west. Through the years the town has changed to suit the tastes and trends of it's would be guests.

We arrived just after eleven back to our hotel, the weekend stag and hens littered the car parks and were spilling out of the various function rooms, with drinks of varying quality and colours. The air was heavy with cigarette smoke, shame and disappointment. Various hens screamed to the odd buck "leave it, leave it, he ain't worth it". It was nice to know that the railway was still making a good living busing the workers in from the Essex coast availing them of the opportunity to have a final bit of practice before they get married. Now more than ever the little red phone box looked out of time, almost red with embarrassment following a parade of body parts varying in beauty heaving against its side, making any 1950's indiscretion seem like the rambling fumbling's of a backwards altar boy.

Chapter Eleven: Two are mad in Dorset

Our final day in Dorset was off to a good start, after a good all you can eat cooked breakfast at the hotel Michaela packed our things with ruthless efficiency and we was on the road to the Isle of Portland at the southernmost tip of the coast, a world heritage site famous for its Portland Stone (a form of limestone) which was used for the construction of many illustrious buildings the most famous of which is St Paul's Cathedral. Portland is also an important area of scientific importance, abundant in rare species of flora and fauna it is a special place whereby if you are lucky you can see its protected sand lizards and the super studded blue butterflies. The author Thomas hardy among other writers set some of his novels in Portland, he wrote affectionately about it. Inspired by its beautiful coastlines, dunes and cliffs he captured the spirit of the place although I doubt that Thomas Hardy cares if I appreciate his work or not.

We had a full day planned, a tour around the Portland lighthouse and a visit to Portland castle followed by a well-deserved dinner in Weymouth. The walks along the dunes were worth the visit alone. The legacies of Portland's naval and military contributions were evident wherever you looked. The castle itself was on the tip of the land overhanging the sea at points, strategically well positioned with views across the channel it was pressed back into service after a hundred and thirty year retirement by the army to support the south coast defences during the Second World War. The Harbour until recent years was used by NATO controlled ships until the mid-nineties when their operations ceased as the world around changed and for a brief spell became a better place.

Since the harbingers of war vacated Portland after a long and valued service the harbour and the beach is now an oasis of tranquillity with some of the best internationally recognised competitive sailing waters in the world, the harbour now a hub of leisure and sailing outlets, with clubs by the dozen all choosing the Bill for its superior tidal currents and air stream. Portland has seen tourism grow in the area and as peace reins in this quiet part of the world the Lighthouse which has stood proudly Since its commissioning in 1906 stood dressed in its traditional red and white patina, just as much an icon of style as it is of engineering draws many adoring crowds from all over the world keen to tread the one hundred and fifty steps to it's top to be rewarded with joyous views of heaven.

Michaela and I made it to the top of the lighthouse, we was indeed rewarded for efforts the calm flat sea lay out before us brilliantly blue, the horizon was undisguisable, a single puffy white cloud hung lonely in the sky, the brilliant heat radiated through the ancient glass stifling my efforts to breathe, we were soon headed back down the stairs breathless from the view, heat and the stairs, as soon as we arrived at the bottom, I took large draft of my well-deserved drink. We held hands as we walked around the visitor centre that was innovative and interesting, I learnt stories of the war efforts and the sacrifices made by the people of Portland who stood resolutely shoulder to shoulder with our army and navy. United in strife and hopefulness as only that generation could.

We walked in the hot sunshine along the shingle towards Portland castle, for the first time in weeks I felt tired, the nervous energy in me seemed to have subsided. I recognized that for the first time in a long time I was relaxed. Michaela noticed my lagging energy and soon had me sat in the small castle café nursing a cup of passable tea. I couldn't explain the sudden lack of energy or what had caused it, Michaela suggested that it might actually be that that I was relaxing and perhaps the mix of constant adrenalin and stress had been propelling me on, a shared thought that seemed to point true. While I had driven more than a thousand miles in just a few days and despite some snatched moments of sleep we had been constantly on the go. I generally never got ill as a rule but as I sat with my tea and cake a memory of my childhood came flooding back to me.

I remembered just barely back to my pre-school years, Cheryl had started school and I had mum all to myself during school hours. Like many people, my memories of this time are few and far between, I can remember being unwell one morning, this was well before the game changing Video recorder proliferated every home in the land. I had waited patiently all morning for my favourite program to grace the screen in all its technicolour glory. I was in love with the Mr Men; everything about it was my favourite. I loved the simple opening theme tune, the easy honeyed tones of Arthur Lowe and bright and tidy world of the Mr Men.

As normal daytime programming finished the lunchtime children's programs ushered themselves in and for almost an hour pre-schoolers all over the country like me sat in contented bliss with jam sandwiches and cups of orange juice. The roster of programs was perfect King Rollo, Button Moon, Chorton and the wheelies complete with Fenella the Kettle joined Jamie and his magic lamp to entertain us. Every child my age has their favourite. The only thing that marred our joy was the looming realisation that the news would soon follow and it would all be over for another day, before the end credits had rolled the remains of jam sandwiches would be left to soak up the spilled orange, knocked to the floor by our flailing un coordinated arms and legs as we fled from the lunchtime news or the dreadfully dull Pebble Mill at one.

I was lucky to live in an age where children's programs were innovative fuelled by the dying embers of the creative and far more permissive minds of television executives freed from the rigid broadcasting protocols of the 50's and 60's that represented a bygone age, the children's television department went through a golden age of creativity and I was lucky enough to be sat right there jam sandwich in hand enjoying its output. Progressive minds had been opened up and free to challenge and explore the young minds in new ways, new techniques and technologies in television production resulted in costs lowering enough to make the creation of new worlds possible guided by a creativity that was not before seen or allowed on children's programming before, now rejecting the status quo new and different concepts were emerging the boundaries were not only pushed they were barely visible, in America Seseme street was reigning supreme over the airwaves and while Jim Henson had a massive hit on his hands with it he struggled to bring us the mania of Kermit, Miss Piggy and the muppets to TV screens in his home country unable to convince any studio to take a chance on him with conservative political agenda playing out across all form of media his now iconic creations at one stage looked like they would never see the light of day. It took the open mindedness of the BBC and the vision and the tireless dedication of Jim Henson to start the music and light the lights creating perhaps one of the most endearing and successful children's franchises of all time.

Away from Seseme Street, planted firmly in Kent I waited as patiently as any pre-schooler could counting down the hours and minutes until the Mr Men arrived on the screen working their simple but spellbinding magic on my tiny little mind. Soon though my fever took hold and before I knew it, I was being woken by my mum, it was three o clock and we needed to go and collect Cheryl from school. The concept of television had not yet fully formed in my mind, I asked mum "if the telly is off, do the programs still happen?" "Yes love" she answered sadly sensing my upset. I remember my disappointment as I explained that I thought if the TV was turned off then the programs couldn't possibly happen, could they? Sadly, mum reaffirmed that I would have to wait until next week for a glimpse of my program. Mum gave me a big hug, despondent I allowed her to treat me to some sweets on the way from the school run and to my joy, I was rewarded with my very own Mr Man comic. My mum was always awesome and looking back it is the culmination of all those precious small moments, her complete understanding of what we were feeling and how to heal us. I learnt as my grief played out and played tricks on me that it was those reassuring seconds where uncertainty was easily banished by her very presence that I miss her most.

The Castle though wasn't going to visit itself, I put thoughts of tiredness behind me. Portland Castle had many things in common with Corfe, although built as an artillery fort on the orders of Henry VIII in 1541 it provided sea defences for several hundred years, it saw action during the Napoleonic wars. Portland like Corfe was a Royalist stronghold, sieged twice in 1647 it resisted once before falling to the parliamentary armies in 1647. Portland to my joy was much unmolested each one room after the next revealed a secret, I was in awe of the engineering and ingenuity that went into the planning and creation of such a vast structure, built through necessity with passion and dedication its functionality surpassed by its beauty. Soon we walked along the turrets looking out towards the channel, we paused and stood the breeze blowing in from the sea was heavy on our shoulders, the waves lashed against the walls scattering a mist of sea spray over the assembled visitors seeking respite from the afternoon sun.

When you go on a journey we all go about it differently, whether we are off to the beach or to see a long distance loved one we all prepare differently, some of us meticulously plan each stop, detailing each rest brake to the nearest minute. Others plan well ahead removing any need to stop at all. Some at a moment's notice hop into the car and go, not worrying about what is ahead. Some worry about the people travelling with them making sure they have the best experience, other put more thought into whether the car will get everyone there safely busily checking the oil and fluids along with the brakes, ensuring the spare wheel is present and correct before they move an inch.

I am often amused that many people are unable to commence any journey of any length for any reason without hard boiled sweets, believing that nothing should be attempted without a humbug for emergencies their only worry being if they got stuck in traffic and the whole family sucked on the sweet in unison would the windows cave in cutting everyone into tiny pieces leaving no option but to have the whole interior professionally valeted. The resulting quandary negated in the mind of the worrier by opening the driver's side window a crack, applying the same logic that jumping in the air just before a plummeting lift hits the bottom of the shaft will save them.

Popular culture, song lyrics and interior design items found in all good pound shops will all attest that life is journey also. We all have different approaches to our journey, some rush in where angels fear to tread, while others lead measured if not meek lives, others follow the rules of religion obsequiously serving their god while being mean and trite to others. Many people spend their lives looking after others, championing the rights of the few. Some of the most interesting people I have met don't have a plan they live life how they see fit, holding themselves accountable to their own values knowing that the outcome of any decision they make will be half chance anyway.

Michaela and I were on our journey together, Life for us was just starting. Our relationship was new and exciting, we were getting to know each other in new ways as each day passed, she amazed me often and my admiration for her was only surpassed by my love. We had been on the road a while, We stopped late morning for a quick rest before our onward journey and we was now resting in the shady pines of a forest, the ancient trees providing us shelter from a summer shower, the whispering sound of the rain rustled through the low branches of the trees, the smell of cut grass mingled with the fresh scent of the rain producing a heady aroma that filled my nostrils transporting me back to endless childhood summers. As we waited for a break in the rain I sat happily reflecting on our last few weeks' worth of adventures.

I was starting to feel more human, every waking moment was no longer painted in darkness, and I didn't spend endless hours sat shut in my own little world, closed off to people and experiences. I had seen some places from my past, places that I had always wanted to see and some places that had surprised and delighted me. I felt for the first time that my mind's thirst for knowledge had started to return. Once again, I was interested in the new and the different. I no longer felt the need to keep looking back and when I did, I found quite often that I did so with a smile. I was damaged absolutely no doubt, but I was willing to carry on moving forwards a small step at a time but a step, nevertheless. With more good days than bad I was under no illusion that grief wasn't done with me just yet, but I felt at least now I understood it. I knew it was a bastard and I knew mum wouldn't want me to give in.

Depending on who you listen to, or what articles you read the experts in grief say there are (depending on where your sensibilities land and how much of an arsehole the expert is) that there are anything between three and ten stages to grief, there are also impressive charts with clever algorithms running through them calculating how long it should take a person to "get over" a death usefully applying parameters such as what relation to you the person you lost was and how long you have known them, this data can then be taken down and mucked around and distilled into many handy and useful pocket guides that can be bought out when needed to fix your friends or loved ones in ten easy steps as one book can fit all. Fuck off. Once you have experienced grief you are an expert whether you like it or not. Your thoughts and opinions all matter, grief doesn't define you it separates you from those that it hasn't touched.

Holding your baby for a brief second of life, seeing something so perfect, so trusting and absolutely right fade away according to some self-appointed self-help books should therefore by the expert's logic be far less painful and traumatic than losing your child when they are thirty by pure rationale that you would have the opportunity to be closer to an older child. This simple comparison disproves so many concepts of time and proximity to a person you have lost. Human emotion is far too complex to be worked through in such a way, the real experts in grief management will tell you, it takes as long as it takes and you will feel what you feel and as frustrating as that is, it's true. No expert, no matter how gifted will cure you of your grief, such things aren't possible, However they can help you to work through your feelings, asking the right questions, in the right order at the right pace to get you to the right answer. No right answer is the same for any two people.

The pain for everyone will be different too, but no more or less, the simple truth is there is no right amount of time, there is no right way to grieve, grief is a journey and it isn't ended by following a process written or otherwise. It is important to take enough time to process what has happened, to let your real feelings out. Some people will want to talk a lot, cry a lot and eat a lot; others may just want to run away. I understood that what I had gone through weren't stages of grief picked from a catalogue but I was grieving, I was reacting in a real emotional way to what had happened, grief is perhaps the truest thing that could happen to a person. It sucks but no matter what you are going through I promise you will get through it; you will tame it no matter how much you think you won't. It will be the hardest thing you will ever do, but if you listen to yourself and take all the time you need, you will heal, and you will remember and you will eventually be able to smile, you will also understand that it is OK to smile and laugh.

In my grief, which I guarded jealously, I knew deep down that I was resisting life, I had needed to put a pause in it, I saw running away as a positive thing to do. I needed to clear my head and take stock of my life, I needed to get away. I often I had the feeling that I had gone mad as if I was living inside a Salvador Dali painting, the lines were clear but not where they should be. My Panic followed my calm as my mind constantly raced from one what if to another. My heart often pounded in my chest, beating like a drum my ears, headaches tore through my skull echoing through my eye sockets shocking my jaw in waves inducing vomit to flow from my mouth and through my nose. You are in the belly of beast; you can see no way out. You are figuratively going through hell, and when you are going through hell the only thing to do is to keep going.

There is no right or wrong, there is only forwards, even if going forwards means that for a time you have to go back, it feels almost impossible to think at times but that is OK, it is more important to feel, to try and listen to your emotions, to understand the nagging voice inside your head as confidence and paranoia can play some terrible tricks on the most rational of minds, the tricks they can play on the bereaved mind however is devastating and the consequences of such can be dire. The mind when in any kind of trauma can be malicious and small, self-doubt; self-loathing and dread become the loneliest and devastating of emotions. Hatred magnifies and manifests itself in the darkest corners of your psyche, it has the power to enslave you for a lifetime if you let it, leaving a person stuck, unable to move on, and bitter in outlook, ending up just as much a ghost as the person they have lost.

One of the most dreadful notions is that of the "what if", a destructive and redundant proposition that can induce madness to epic proportions. "What if they had spotted the lump earlier" or "what if I told her to go to the doctor?" The most miserable of statements the what if, it is as useful as the desire to have the use of a time machine. No good will come from such thoughts, even so they are part of what makes us human. Depression is a factor that grief brings into play, I accepted eventually through talking to Michaela that I was depressed, I just didn't know it at first. Initially I thought depression was mine to deal with and conquer, I was though starting to see that Michaela saw it as something different, to her it was a battle best fought with two and slowly I began to understand that I had become we.

The first trick my mind played on me was to tell me that I wasn't depressed, that I must be making it all up. You think, I can't be depressed as I'm not sat around in my dressing gown and I'm not crying every two minutes. I can do my job just fine and I'm coping. Depression is far more dangerous than that, it lies in wait for its prey drawing you in, it convinces you to think that building defensive walls internally will help, that talking will be no good, it convinces you that all is well. The second trick and by far the most dangerous is it tries to convince you that no one will be interested in listening to you, it relies on isolating you from your friends and family, it wants you to withdraw from your life. Depression plays by no rules it will attack a millionaire rock star and a lorry driver the same way, its strength is silence. It doesn't kill you, but it will happily take your life. Through talking to people and being honest about my depression I managed to beat it, I have been free from it for nearly five years. Never be fooled, talking about how you are feeling is the first step to recovery, people are amazing and the response I received from my friends and my family is a testament to how great the human race can be.

Chapter Twelve: Cornish pasties and a cream tea please!

The journey west was a leisurely one, we soon had Dorset in our rear-view mirror, and we were soon in Devon, with an opportunity for a real Devonshire Tea I was soon scanning the green and pleasant lands for signs of a tea shop. I also had a mounting desire for some cider, we had arrived in the right place and I couldn't wait. The people of Devon are obsessed county wide by the humble Cornish pasty, unlike the Pavlova and the Bakewell tart Devon is happy to let Cornwall take the credit. The pasty originated from the tin mines of Cornwall, originally filled on one side with savoury goodness and with a sweet apple filling on the other encrusted in pastry with a thick crust that enabled the miners to eat safely in the dark gloom of the mine holding the pasty by the thick crust keeping the poisonous tin residue from their hands well away from their stomachs. Cornwall is littered with old mines, some of which are now heritage centres celebrating the history of the industry, others now long gone are marked only by the rubble that still remains in the vast expanse of beautiful moorlands, hills and valleys.

The South West is a very special place, it is host to some of the friendliest and best people I have ever met it has an abundance of natural beauty and rare wildlife species in spades. In the summer visitors in their droves arrive at the Devon and Cornwall coasts to experience the sights while spending their precious leisure time exploring everything the West Country has to offer. From Arthurian legend to ancient battles and invasions the West Country has it all.

We were due to stay in Falmouth for a few days, which would allow us to explore the best of Cornwall before heading back up towards Devon for a good explore, I admit I was excited, I felt relaxed and the weather made everything seem possible. The Hot August sunshine blended like cider with the West Country air creating a soothing feeling in my soul, capable of singing you to sleep when you least expected it (much like the local scrumpy).

Michaela was dressed in her pretty white summer dress, I regarded her, she had caught the sun and her skin looked almost Mediterranean against the cotton straps of her top. She beamed back at me, nothing was said but we understood each other, we were happy, and I knew I wanted to be with her forever.

As the Green of Devon peeled away to the browns of Cornwall we headed towards St Michael's mount a tidal island near and linked to Marazion on the Cornish coast, If you catch the tide right you can still walk across the causeway straight onto the island itself. The Island was gifted to the Order of Mont Saint-Michel by Edward the confessor in the Eleventh century although it's links to the monastery date back several hundred years earlier, Now like many of the coastal regions in the south and south west the island itself is designated a site of geological importance ably looked after by the National trust and the owners, who have been there since 1650 the St Aubyn family have guarded and cherished the place with the reverence it deserves, the name of the mount in the Cornish language (yes they like the Welsh have their own) translates simply as "the rock in the wood" many of the ancient trees have long since surrendered to the waters but still remain to be seen at low tide.

The island itself is beautiful beyond words, When we landed on the rock I was instantly taken aback as to how unspoilt the island was, given that it was fortified during world war two as part of the sea defence network in 1941, I understood immediately and expected the rumoured stories to be true that according to recent reports from recently unearthed war time files that Nazi foreign minister (read major league arsehole) Joachim Von Ribbentrop planned after the war to have the island all to himself as his home. Von Ribbentrop a former German ambassador to Britain had been a firm advocate (read tosspot) of an Anglo-German alliance before the war, thankfully he never got his hands on St Michael's instead his claim to fame was to be the first person convicted of war crimes at Nuremberg to be hanged (after Hermann Goring, like Hitler cowardly took his own life) after being Captured by the Belgian SAS he sent rambling and begging letters to various members of state in the UK but his fate was sealed and The Rock remained an arsehole free haven of peace and tranquillity for all those that have had and still have the privilege and freedom to visit.

We made our way around the island, taking in the beautiful coastal views, the heat was fierce and just down the road in Falmouth the temperature was already hitting thirty degrees, cooling breezes swept in from the sea giving us welcome respite that came through in waves of utter bliss. I have always loved history and I was in awe of the few that changed the course of world history, Lamenting as to how things could have been so different I drank in the view like it was water, consuming until the point of drowning. It's a special place indeed, Michaela and I have a picture of the mount that Michaela took, it is printed onto a giant canvas and hangs proudly on our living room wall next to one she took of Whitby Abbey (the Abbey's story I'll tell you later).

We made our way to the Chapel Rock, the site of a small shrine dedicated to the Virgin Mary, where many people pause to worship, not being of any religious persuasion we paused to show our respect for those that did and made our way up the mount to the castle, after a look around we made our way to the harbour where the first footprint of Queen Victoria is preserved in brass when she made a visit here in 1846, a short distance away on the little bowling green the footprint of King Edward the seventh can be seen from his visit, these simple pleasures delighted me, saved from the erosion of an over exploited tourist trap The mount is lucky to remain as it was, for me it is an under visited jewel in England's wonderful heritage, I have a lot of love for this little piece of

England and my hat goes off to the national trust for keeping it this way.

As the afternoon sun burned high in the sky, we made our way towards Lands' End. I had wanted to travel the length of the country and I was filled with a certain amount of achievement when I was finally stood at the Lands' End marker, Michaela dutifully took my photograph and after a few selfies together I felt like millennial. We sat in the world's End pub and enjoyed some of the finest cider that the county could offer fondly referred to by the locals as spread eagled lady (dedicated to the effects that two halves of the stuff could have on one) we was suitably refreshed, a friend who knows Land's End well had told me about the best walking path around the cliffs, giving the best views, with camera in hand and swelling cider bellies we set off in search of history.

My links with Cornwall stretch back more than thirty years, my good friend Christian and I would holiday in Cornwall each year, each year the journey would be full of the never realized ambition to get well and truly fucked in a really hot way, however the reality was sadly that the only hot thing was the copious amounts of tea we drank and the only thing that got fucked was the inflatable Cadillac lido that burst as I tried to alight it while staying cool in front of swarms of teenage girls that adorned Fistral Beach, after being dragged along the bottom of the sea and almost drowning I was sure a life lesson about showing off should have been learnt, sadly for everyone our show boating and lack of sex lasted the whole of the holiday.

Chris and I had had some great days, like with my school holiday with the gang from Tubbenden our last holiday in Cornwall together came when we was fifteen, we were both at a cross roads in life, secondary school for us was finished and the bond of school that held us together was no more and the prospect of not seeing each other every day upset me, I thought that Chris and I would eventually drift apart like many friendships do, to my absolute joy we are to this day still great friends.

The early nineties was a funny time to be a teenager, the world was changing, AIDS wasn't still entirely understood and the music was in total melt down, the charts a melting pot of rock, heavy metal, rap and dance, no genre was defining our generation like glam rock had done in the seventies and new wave in the eighties. Own clothes day at our school was like a boot fair in an acid factory (also a type of music that assaulted us when we weren't looking) there was chinos, lumberjack shirts, ted baker tops, tie dyed tops and denim everywhere. Our style was eclectic to say the least; we lived in fear that at any moment Bez from the happy Mondays would jump out of a wardrobe mid trip and shake his maracas in your face, ruining any chance of a chemical romance. It was a happy carefree time for us.

One thing that kept Chris and I going through the last term of school was our final holiday to Cornwall, we had planned our usual program of odd jobbing for the first half of the holiday to earn some money before setting off in the back of Christian's mum's car. We tried unsuccessfully at many things to earn some money, car washing, cleaning and the odd spot of gardening, feeling defeated each year invariably we would be handed a job out of pity by Christian's aunt. So, after a week or so of decorating we had fifteen crisp twenty-pound notes in our hands each. More than enough for a gallivant around the west country.

After what seemed like an ice age our holiday finally started, We stayed in Christian's Grandad's holiday home in Par, a pretty harbour village on the east coast, complete with a little village pub with a fragrant and almost militant disregard for the licensing laws which we happily flouted along with them before falling over backwards, thankfully never out of a window. Our addiction to Cider was intense but fleeting, there was an embarrassing blue tongued incident with a couple of local girls, a belt and a bottle of Curacao, when after several large net glasses of devil's piss Christian, blue tongued and wobbling made a heartfelt appeal to whip each one with his belt spanking his hand playfully as he did so, following not our first rejection that night, but certainly our last Christian suddenly announced that his balls were hot as slid down the wall for the ten count.

Being rather pissed and blue tongued myself, my options were limited, as no one was up for a spanking with a belt or otherwise and being a man down the only option left open to me was surrender. I have a history when drunk of falling backwards, and as I joined Christian on the ground we both laid still in the cool air, the sky was brilliant with stars and as we gazed up in our alcoholic haze we almost definitely saw an alien spacecraft, the anal probing from the aliens was nothing compared to the welcome we got the next morning when we awoke and presented ourselves to Christian's panic stricken mum.

Running away was fast proving to be the tonic that I needed, I found increasingly that I was looking back to my childhood and the people that linked me, I was looking for connections to an easier and more innocent time in my life, when mum was well and I was happy. The grieving process is complex at best and I understood that the need to look back was part of dealing with life now and in the future, the one thing I was certain of was the need I had to connect with friends and family, it was an oxymoron in a way because at the same time I had no desire to talk about my mum. I had removed all pictures of her, which in retrospect seems odd to me now. I remembered when my Uncle died my aunt had pictures of him all over the house; there is no right way to grieve and no right way to support someone that is. The most important thing is that if someone can't see the bright side, sit a while with them in the dark sometimes that is all they need. No talking, no cheering. Just someone to be there.

As we walked around the cliffs the wonder of Lands' End was endless, Old harry and his wife paled by comparison, Michaela's camera clicked and zipped as we found beauty at every turn, I reassured myself that mum would have liked it here. I missed her, a sense of sorrow came over me, only just and very fleeting but it was there. I walked over to Michaela and sat on a nearby rock, instinctively Michaela came and sat next to me, in silence under the hot august sunshine we sat in the dark for a while looking out towards the Atlantic Ocean, an arched rock formation glistened as the sea crashed against it, called the song of the sea the formation looked stunning as the sun moved behind the formation of the rocks the archway like my mood lit up in spectacular fashion, I sensed urgency in the moment and urged Michaela to capture it all with her camera, it clicked twice, the resulting pictures hang proudly in our home. The artist Turner painted this very scene and a few years later I was delighted to see it hanging in the Tate gallery, a moment frozen in time captured by two artists in two mediums more than hundred years apart. Nothing there had changed it was almost identical, I like to think that seeing the Turner painting hanging resplendent, its place in art history well established was serendipity, every picture tells a story.

We spent a quiet evening in Cornwall soaking up the Cider while dining on the most beautiful steaks that I have ever tasted, Falmouth in the summer is a wonderful place to be. The Quay was alive with families enjoying the summer evening. Pleasure boats swarmed with happy holiday makers arriving and departing in equal measure from tours of the Fal River and the coast beyond. Children ran and mothers screamed, this corner of England knew bliss.

Cornwall is a happy place, it has a sense of contentment and for me it is filled with memories of my teens and driven by the desire to make many more memories I sat watching the boats rise and fall on the water, running away had never been more peaceful. I watched as a little girl dressed in a pretty pink and blue dress skipped along the cobbles lagging intentionally ever so slightly behind the rest of her family. Her hair was blonde as could be, almost spun gold in colour she was half her mum, half her dad but completely and undeniably herself. Her blue eyes trailed a little boy carrying a bright red balloon, her eyes flitted from the boy to balloon and back again. A big smile spread across her face as she waved to the boy who curtly poked his tongue out at her. The little girl's face dropped the hurt apparent in her eyes, she caught my gaze and I smiled at her in an instant her smile returned, and she waved to me, I waved back much to her delight. I was rewarded with the most beautiful little laugh.

As soon as this little dot had arrived and taken her seat at the table with her family she had become my friend, waving and playing peekaboo with me at every opportunity, her face lit up when her ice cream arrived and she set about it like a starving wolf. Michaela and I settled our bill and got ready to head back to our hotel, as I turned to leave, I waved goodbye to my new little friend, calling out at the top of her voice she said goodbye. Life is just a series of moments, each one more precious than the last. We are all destined to leave this world, all at different times and in different ways. We are simply queuing, never knowing who is next. This little girl was making each of her moments special, embracing everything that was good, although upset she took the little boy rejecting her offer of fleeting friendship in her stride, she moved on and opened herself up to the next experience not letting one thorn ruin her day, she offered her friendship freely and I was certain that this little girl with all her hopes and dream would become in time a woman of vision and value. I saw in her a pioneer and the mystery that I will never know is as exciting to me as her life will be for her.

Children don't hate learning in fact I'm sure the opposite is true. Children hate being intimidated and confused by the subject, not the act of learning. The beauty of raising a child is everything is a journey, the world they inherit is theirs to explore moment by moment and if nurtured they will find their passion and they will be incredible. Children should be our passion.

Knowing your own self-worth is important, nobody owes you the luxury of being happy, you make your own happiness and what we accept is what we get, at three years old this little girl had nailed it, she had moved on and found happiness and friendship elsewhere, she was officially my hero. Life for her was not complicated, it was sweet and simple someone gives you the finger? Fuck them off and move on. I think how far you get in life in terms of happiness and respect centres on how you treat the young, the vulnerable and the old, if you are lucky and you live life to the full you will have enough moments to be all three yourself.

Our meal done I was feeling well fed and my bed was calling me, we had a final walk around the harbour and started the climb up the steep hill towards our hotel, aided by cider I happily swayed in unison with the sea breeze, as we reached the top of the hill we turned to face the sea, the waves crashed against the port stones, seagulls ducked and dived, pouncing on the craps of uneaten food and discarded rubbish. They cried and screeched to each other shouting out where the best morsels can be found.

Chapter Thirteen: Devon knows it's creamy

We travelled towards Dartmoor national park, the weather was much cooler than it had been, the fierce heat of the sun had relented, and we enjoyed the respite. We soon reached the outskirts of Dartmoor for a few days of Devon goodness, I soon realised being new and unfamiliar with Dartmoor that you could spend an entire two-week holiday here and still not get around to seeing everything. The first point of order was to finally have a cream tea that I had been lusting after, we arrived in the little village of Ashburton where we made a beeline for the nearest little tea room, spoilt for choice and blissfully happy we tucked into our tea and cream (cream first then the jam, we always do thing properly). We spent a few happy hours walking the gift and antique shops that adorn the pretty streets.

As the sunshine triumphed, we walked along the river dart, we stood watching the canoes travelling past, and the rush of the water and the excited sound of children's laughter filled the air. Our main destination was the famous Dartmoor prison, completed and opened in 1809 the prison was built to hold prisoners of the Napoleonic war, owned by the Duchy of Cornwall it is operated not as its reputation would have you believe but as a low security prison housing mainly white collar and low risk prisoners, the sight of the prison just outside of Princetown is indeed imposing and impressive. Designated a grade two listed building in 1987 the prison has its very own museum set in the former diary buildings opposite the main prison.

The prison has a colourful political and social history being the resting place of over two hundred and seventy prisoners, many of whom were soldiers killed illegally and without a great deal of reason The British government of the time later paid reparations to the families of the victims . After the war ended the prison was initially closed reopening again as a criminal prison in 1850. One of the prison's most infamous was friend of the Kray twins Frank "Mad Axeman" Mitchell, who while imprisoned at Dartmoor in 1966 Mitchell was working in a small gang of convicts on the moors, he disappeared and was spirited away by members of the Kray gang. Never one to be accused of having sense and logic Mitchell while on the run and in hiding in East London under the protection of the Kray twins he became more and more difficult to control, realising their mistake the only way out for the Krays was to have Mitchell killed.

On Christmas Eve 1966 Mitchell was led into the back of a van, met by members of the gang he was shot twelve times, wrapped in chicken wire and unceremoniously dumped in the English Channel, His body was never recovered, the only thing known is he never returned to Dartmoor. Eventually Ron Kray and members of his gang were tried but never convicted for his murder although in 1996 Freddie Foreman, one of the original gang members accused of Mitchell's murder controversially admitted to killing Mitchell as a favour to Ron Kray, however the double jeopardy laws prohibited him from being tried again. Ron regarded Mitchell as a side note, merely someone that he made the mistake of helping, the price of that help proved fatal.

Eleven miles to the north east of Dartmoor prison through the little town of Tavistock, is Brentor church, an isolated church situated on the top of a large extinct volcano. With no made path or road to the church many a bride has made the trip to her wedding in wellies, an idea that I love the thought of. The church sits high on the Tor and the views across the moors are breath taking. The wild heather grows as freely as the wild moor ponies run, as I surveyed the land thoughts of Sherlock Holmes and his hounds sprang to mind as we drove the moor roads towards Somerset, the roads were glorious and an experience in themselves never had rugged looked so beautiful, the road rose and fell almost as much as it twisted and turned. Fast stretches of open road soon gave way to small villages and hamlets, with our windows down and our music playing the Devon air rushed us, Devon air has the restorative qualities to clear your lungs and your head, it can ease you into sleep and wake you up like an unlimited supply of medicine on a boundless tap good for whatever ills you.

We soon crossed into Somerset arriving at Cheddar Gorge a little after two in the afternoon, We walked through the little gorge its treelined rocky cliffs rising on each side of the small high street, towards the bottom of the steep hills is a little lake with a small wooded island in the middle, a short hop over a little bridge takes you into the village.

As we climbed hill towards Cox cave we stopped to watch a carnival of ducks as parading down the Cheddar Yeo river, the waterway was still and calm, we followed it up hill towards its source at Gough cave, soon the still water gave way to a small waterfall, little birds mingled with the ducks catching crane flies that were brave enough to venture close.

The day was hot, we stopped at a small café enjoying an ice cream each as we watched the water dance, children ran around on the grassy banks, dogs ran happily along the long narrow paths, each one showing an intense interest in the ducks as their owners looked on nervously fearing their pet may enter the water on a duck hunt, secretly I think many of the parents were worrying about the same. Everyone seemed to be enjoying their family time in the sun.

There was a plan to build a cable car from the gorge basin up to the top of the south cliff at one stage in the Gorge's history in an attempt to attract more visitors. I thought back to the cable chairs at the Needles and felt slightly defensive of this beautiful place, I was glad that the plan had been quashed, the good old national trust objecting fearing that the Gorge would resemble a theme park rather than a place of historical, natural and archaeological importance. As I drank in the views, I was grateful all over again to the national trust as their lobbying had saved this place with its incredible views and attractions. They do stunning work not just managing houses and properties but protecting our heritage from ourselves.

We spent a few happy hours visiting the caves, the air was cool, there was a moisture in the air that in many ways felt unique, stalagmites rose up from the cool water pools thousands of years in the making. I was soon nursing an extreme case of paranoia as Stalactites hung precariously close to my head as I walked a snail's pace, I desperately tried to avoid being the subject of the local newspaper headlines that evening, I could see it now "moron attacks thousand year old relic".

To be considered a genuine Cheddar cheese it has to be made within thirty miles of Wells Cathedral and be made with delicious Devon or Somerset milk. I was surprised to learn though that it doesn't enjoy any formal heritage status like Champagne and other regionally specialized foods, this omission allows any manufacturer to call their cheese Cheddar even if it has never been in Somerset county let alone the Cheddar Gorge itself. To assert the quality and protect the honour of the genuine cave cheese the local producers created a pedigree of Cheddar cheese branded "west County farmhouse Cheddar" which assures any cheese fan that their cheese on toast is of the highest order sent with love from this beautiful corner of Somerset.

As our eyes adjusted from the humid, dark cool caves we stepped back onto the beautifully appointed high street, Somerset Cider, whiskey and fudge was abundantly and proudly displayed in the neatly lined shop windows. We headed towards the West county farmhouse cheddar shop and tasted the samples along with the most delicious pickles and chutneys, confused as to what the difference between the two was it soon became clear that it was polite not to ask as no one else seemed to know either, it was like I had exposed a dirty secret only it was me that was a bastard.

Thirty pounds lighter and thirsty from the salty goodness of the cheese we walked a few short steps to the neighbouring Whiskey shop where happily we sampled their wares, the whiskey was phenomenal, but not being much of a drinker I couldn't justify the price of a fine bottle of Somerset's finest, Michaela found a very agreeable scrumpy which we bought to accompany our cheese later. Feeling happy if not slightly giddy we started our climb to the top of the gorge along the cliffs, cursing my disorganisation the weight of the various cheeses, scrumpy and sweets was making we sweat and pant in a rather porn star sort of manner.

Thoughts of collapsing in a heap holding my heart while ascending to the summit which was now looking like a million miles off filled my head. I laughed to myself at the thought of being scooped up and when arriving in hospital suffering a heart attack, the finest medical minds are gathered around me, diligently working through the night to find out what has ailed me, the forensic team are summoned and as they go through my bags the mystery is solved, "the git has bags full with a shit load of cheese, booze, fudge and sweets" the bugger deserves it "give him another shot with defibrillator dolly, teach the fucker a lesson…while you're at it pump some castor oil up his arse!".

We eventually arrived at the top of the north cliffs, hot and bothered we stopped for a rest and some lunch, the cheese samples now well and truly worked off and a distant memory. We sat in the sun eating our picnic, the gorge spread out before us. It felt peaceful, I thought to myself Somerset had it all, the scenery, the caves, scrumpy and Cheese.

Goats lined the paths and wandered along the sides of the steep cliffs they made their way along the rocky precipices looking for the most delicious and longest grasses. Happily, they bleated and shit on the cars parked far below, the odd one I thought must occasionally tumble off the cliff side. I wondered if some poor sod had ever met their maker as goat took them by surprise unceremoniously landing on their head, it would I lamented be worse to see it coming towards you, your last moments on earth spent witnessing goat anus hurtling towards you before it all goes dark. I made a mental note to ask a guide if I saw one what the ratio of goats bouncing off of unsuspecting tourists heads is, I'm sure it would be much lower than the amount of goats that bounce off the bonnet of your car, As we pulled out of the car park and headed north to Shropshire a bright yellow 2CV headed towards us, I crossed my fingers and hoped for goat.

After a wonderful night's sleep we woke refreshed just after six in the morning, our heads hinted at memories of cider and good food, we had driven the short distance from Cheddar Gorge to a little bed and breakfast outside the village, surrounded by fields accompanied by the morning chorus we gathered ourselves together ready for another day on the road.

I had liked Somerset far more than I thought I would with its villages, streams and fields it had a little bit of everything and something for everyone. The people were good and honest, and the friendliness seemed to be baked into their beings making up a part of their DNA. It was a good place, an honest place that I had more than attachment if not an affinity with. Although I was now ready to leave, I was certain I would be back.

Chapter Fourteen: and we tell them!

After a good few hours on the road we arrived in Telford and as was now the new normal we was absolutely starving we headed to the nearest pub from our hotel, running away was a hungry business and the day had been long. We were to spend the next five days in the beautiful Shropshire countryside before heading across country lines to explore wales in all its beauty. I remembered the joy of seeing horse shoe falls for the first time as our barge turned the corner of the canal, the clip clopping of the horse's hooves drawing us giving way to the rustle of grass under his feet as he dipped his head to smell the long absent grass, with elation thoughts of the mighty steam train came thundering back to me, the thrill of feeling the engine shunt out of the Wharf station pushing plumes of triumphant smoke from its dusty throat as it gained speed taking our gang onwards to glory, precious memories each one. I could barely hide my excitement or contain the boy within me.

 As the sun shone down the birds sang as fellow diners happily went about their evening chatting and laughing, feeling relaxed we ate well dining on enormous hamburgers that dripped cheese and oil in equal delicious measures. Onions cascaded down from our burgers splashing to a halt on our plates and clothes.

Full and content we explored the pretty lanes and villages that dominate the beautiful landscape worthy of any picture postcard or Constable painting, I felt like I was in God's own country which I'm told is actually an accolade reserved Yorkshire, I'm sure that Yorkshire wouldn't mind sharing that honour just this once. A few weeks later I was to find out for myself that Yorkshire is equally as beautiful.

The sun began to set in the summer sky, the bright blue expanse above me made me feel small but connected. In many ways it all felt like home. We retired to our hotel I was eager to plan the next few days like a schoolboy gain I was excited to be going back to see Ironbridge and the gorge and to once again be transported back in time walking the streets of Blist's Hill. After a few glasses of wine and beer in the hotel bar we sank into a contented sleep fit for any boy riding the river and the rails.

I awoke with a start to find Michaela absent from my side, already having a head start on me she was already anxious to start our adventures and Blist's Hill awaited us. Michaela was the organised one of us, she kept the wheels on and still does. She is perfect in every way making sure that everyone is fed, watered and has everything they need. After a reasonable breakfast of bacon, sausage and eggs we was soon in the car and without ever hitting 88 miles an hour I was transported back to the future.

The gates of Blist's Hill were as I remembered them although I was sure they were smaller than they had been when I saw them last through the window of our school coach on cue Jason Tate our school joker (he still is a one to this day) let off his customary fart to ensure a rapid and efficient evacuation of the coach. In a haze of noxious fumes consisting of last night's custard and this morning's green eggs mixed with a soupçon of anticipation. We hurried off the bus with our noses buried deep beneath our shirts. As playground law dictated as soon as our hyperactive little feet hit terra firma we started the desperate task of finding and then almost immediately ditching our pre-allocated partners while calling each other mongies and punching each other in the arm in order to spend the day tethered to our friends rather than the nose picker, grass or killjoy. Soon the teacher's call for us to line up in our pairs and stop being ignoramuses lit the touch paper for us all to avoid the clear and present danger of being the one put in a group of three like a third wheel wanker and everyone knew that the third wheel must have something peculiar about them to be feared and avoided (unlucky Brian Scutts, he was just too slow, and like Mrs Simpson said would probably end up in jail a bitter disappointment to his parents).

Mrs Simpson was a teacher and a lady from a bygone age she was painfully thin, it looked like she had two walnuts for breakfast, licked an apple for lunch and dinner was just shouting at a naked picture of herself, she was equally as thin lipped and uptight in posture with wire rimmed glasses framing her gaunt looks, I suspected that in private her reflection troubled her. She was always dressed in a black or white twinset with no hint of colour or personality.

She pined for the good old days when she could give us a good smack across the hand, head or wherever her aim cared to take her, she wasn't mean in the classic sense but she was tough as old boots and had a face that looked like she had trod on an upturned erroneous plug locked in a cycle of pain that digested with relish, She always seemed to have a yearning to be allowed to beat just a few of us, the bit that we never understood about a lady of such standing was that she would layer mountains of make up over herself, drawing her eyebrows on and accentuating her thin tight lips with fuck me now red lipstick painted on with a mortar board, this you understand wasn't a bit of slap it was a definite right hook.

Eventually all the childhood politics had played out and we successfully lined up in our twos just in time to watch Richard throw up his last night's custard all down the back of Alison and all up the front of his shirt, protesting and siting the afore mentioned fart as the root cause of his illness, to the absolute delight and rapture of the rest of the group, Jason (who loved to punch noses so you had to treat him with a bit of care) spurred us on with a rousing rendition of the old school favourite and now sadly defunct playground chant of nice one Cyril, nice one son, nice one Cyril let's have another one, followed shortly when Mrs Simpson was out of earshot with he's a wanker, he's a wanker!

Eventually after various aspersions and recriminations had been flung far and wide we turned to the important task of sorting out who was a wanker and whose mum was fat, Richard was nicely changed into the teachers stunning set of spare clothes that must have been purchased from the London Fire Brigades fire retardant range, basking in a glorious orange T-shirt and a stunning pair of brown girls flannel shorts, while Alison sported a pair of boys shorts and a scowl. It was all tears and snot.

Mrs Simpson looked like she wanted to beat someone just for minute, just for once and as her far away longing look rescinded Richard and the rest of the group was ready for the off but sadly for Richard his new style and attire began to draw comparisons to the similarity of his look to that of the World Cup Willy mascot, we realised then that things were going to get rough for Richard so we did what any good friends would do and abandoned him, denying ever being his friends and after all if he was going to be beaten it made no sense to be caught in the crossfire.

Soon we was all sat on the grass bank flanked by frustrated Blist's Hill tour guides and volunteers who had now joined us as much to police the situation as to entertain us meanwhile Richard finished sobbing and was having his nose blown on some second hand tissue of unknown origin, Jason meanwhile was being spoken to by the deputy head as some noses had been punched while debate raged, melee and excitement reined, my gang really were ace and to our delight we all had survived the politics and the warfare that was involved in exiting the coach.

Without as much Drama Michaela and I walked past the bank, it was still the same, the grass was tall and well-kept I noticed that butterflies danced around the occasional flowers. I smiled at the memory as Michaela grasped my hand we went on our way. For second, I longed for my childhood.

I was transported back in time both figuratively and literally, a willing traveller looking for his future in the past and as we transcended the busy modern world into the recreated Victorian village, it was I was stunned to see still as I remembered it and I was elated, my childhood memories and desperate need for nostalgia hadn't blinded me and nothing felt small or kitsch about the place. I was dizzy with excitement and I grasped Michaela's hand as I almost fell into a run. The sun was bright, and sky was blue it was a perfect setting for a perfect day.

The cobbled streets and faithfully restored houses remained as I had left them and still they were every bit a sight to behold as I remembered, we walked the long high street peering through the beautifully crafted shops stopping to stroke the horses and take in the history as characters dressed in period costume went about their business, a policeman wished us a good morning as we passed happily munching on newly purchased Victorian era sweets from the village store. It was a pause in the hustle and bustle of the previous day and the peace was welcome.

I soon stumbled upon the place I was dying to see and there it was nestled on the corner of the lane the lamppost outside lit and glowing as I remembered it stood Thomas Trevor Chandlers excitedly I walked through the door and I instantly became caught in its melancholy and I longed to be back there running and laughing carefree with my friends and as the past echoed all around me I became a little overwhelmed the thick air caught in my throat and stung my eyes, they watered slightly although I'm not sure whether it was the dust or the memories that caught me off guard. Sadness passed over me that I couldn't explain. It was fleeting but profound.

My mind drifted and I remembered handing over 6 candles wrapped tightly in newspaper by the Chandler's assistant to mum as a gift when I got home and how she pretended to appreciate them as if she had been handed the crown jewels and then later like all the best mums do while then when out of eyesight disposing of the offending frogs, worms or old candles. To my surprise many years later when we was clearing out mums things and sharing sentimental items between us while swapping favourite stories of mum there was inside an old suitcase wrapped tightly in newspaper were six Chandler's candles preserved perfectly and stowed with the care and love you would give to the crown jewels.

My partner Lee and I (luckily in the fight from the coach I had ditched Karl) pushed our way to the front of the counter as the chandler told us the history of candle making which didn't altogether thrill us until Geoffrey decided to follow our ancestors and started tucking into the candle with gusto forcing in large bits of candle, sadly though no longer made with tallow it began to lodge in his throat. It was at this point that I think Mrs Simpson decided to give up teaching before she gave up on life. Twitching and embroiled with rage Mrs Simpson decided not to let Geoffrey die, although it seemed she was weighing up her options and then suddenly with gusto of her own she perhaps decided a court case wasn't her suit and started violently pounding Geoffrey on his back inducing a small thin lipped smile that just lasted long enough to require another drum of lip stick to be applied, her smile soon turned to dismay as Geoffrey stopped going blue which pleased Geoffrey but made Mrs Simpson seem almost sad but comforted in the knowledge that she had avoided a death on her watch she soldiered on her steady path to early retirement.

Each morning before we set out on the coach on our adventures we was required to line up to collect our lunch that was carelessly thrown together by a crack commando unit of monkeys, I said to Lee as we stood queuing for our small rations of prison inspired fodder that this place was ace and when I was older I would definitely come back. He affirmed his appreciation of the place and here we were the furthest we had ever been from home joined together in the spirit of adventure. We all forgave the bad food that week as the prospect of being away was just too exciting for us all.

We walked around Blists Hill the strict paring of twos became more and more liberal as the day progressed and before long the gang was all together in the endless easy sunshine our small minds blown at the sheer scale of the place, the real buses, steam trains and animals made the whole place even more special for us, even Jason forgot about an earlier promise he had made to punch Daniel Hope's nose. We walked through the main high street rode on the horse and carts and watched the specially laid on events, eventually we all arrived at the blacksmiths for our last scheduled event of the day, we was to watch the horseshoes being made in the traditional way that many are still made today, The air was heavy and the smoke from the brazier clung to our clothes and sent streams of tears down our faces and snot to our noses. The final treat for the day was to be a whole hour in the fun fair with the rides and stalls, like many things when you are a child the hour soon passed, and we were ushered onto the coach tired any weary. As we drove from Blists to our lodgings I could have sworn I saw Mrs Simpson smile a secret smile. In a cloud of farts, the coach shook violently and carried us back to our lodgings.

Like the sun rising from slumber and clearing away the early morning fog I vividly remembered my day, the sights and sounds lingered as my adult mind unfolded them and sorted them neatly in to order We can all learn from the past and although it is a great place to hide sometimes it can be almost harmful to linger there to long, looking back instead of forwards is a gamble and as much as we would all like to pause the world sometimes we must journey on through, it is important to maintain the relationships with our siblings and our childhood friends as they are an undeniable link to what was and if you are blessed you will in adulthood have enough of them around still to create a future.

As I stumbled from my memories, Michaela suggested we grab something to eat, she was a little confused by my assertion that we shouldn't have candles or anything made by a convict, having grown used to my unique flavour of humour she batted not one eyelid as pulled me towards the fish and chip shop, already she knew me well and knew me best.

The day past by quickly and soon long shadows formed encircling us weary travellers, the day had been everything I wanted, Michaela and I ambled to the exit half hobbling with tired feet but happy hearts. I had come back, and providence had seen me alright, full of hope I was excited all over again at the prospect of an expedition to Wales and my cherished Llangollen.

Chapter Fifteen: Llangollen Horse Trials

The radio roared as we headed towards Llangollen, Michaela's hair blew in the wind as fresh air and sunshine filled the car from the open window. The fields were lush and green the hills rolled by easily as the road took us through villages and over streams; we had stopped earlier for our now customary breakfast of eggs, bacon and sausages with a bucketful of tea and enough toast to cover a football pitch. The day felt easy and my spirits were high, as we neared the end of the A5 Llangollen in all its glory flowed majestically into sight.

We walked through the town and eventually we was met with the breath taking Afon Dyfrdwy or to me the magnificent river Dee, one of the most beautiful waterways I have ever seen, The following day we were heading to the impressive and equally inspiring Pontcysyllte Aqueduct but for now we gazed into the water and drank the air and the sights in. Michaela was instantly besotted and enchanted with Llangollen and her love affair with the place is only equalled by my own.

We soon found a small hotel by the river side and seated ourselves outside on its decking, the river rushed by and the water beat a soothing tune as it passed over the rocks, ducks swam and ducked away from a gang of newly arrived swans and life couldn't be better, I could almost feel my watch slowing down as we watched the gentle hum of life go by us, after our coffee we headed over the river and began the expedition up Wharf Hill and with a little puff still remaining we reached the canal side the trees hung low over the water and I was taken aback how different the place looked through adult eyes as canal boats lay in the calm water and bees and birds busied themselves around the banks, as a child I had missed all the beauty compelled by the excitement of boarding the canal boat with my gang.

Come on everyone, exclaimed Daniel Humphries lets go watch the horse do a shit, excited and in a frenzy we all rushed towards the stable gates and on que we was rewarded with a loud release of gas, (horse, not Jason) followed by a huge dollop of country gold, Jason in ecstasy declared it a most triumphant piece of shit of the highest order and stopped just short of fainting with joy backwards into the water.

Mark Holland or stinky fingers as we used to call him (more on that later) was a boy that always had neat hair and wore glasses so you couldn't beat him up as often as you would want overheard us rejoicing and enjoying the sights and smells of the welsh countryside and affirmed that he was going to tell Mrs Simpson on us for being rude and disgusting and bringing the reputation of the whole school into disrepute, after inviting him to go forth and be fruitful (not in those words though) Jason offered to punch his nose for him or bath his smelly fingers in the canal. Mark instantly retaliated by bursting into tears and screaming that he wished we was all dead at the top of his voice which soon garnered the attention of Mrs Simpson who thundered across the tow path to us demanding tom know what had gone on, her annoyance turning to anger as she trod in horse crap that had been lovingly dropped on the top path just like in the olden days.

After we were all done exerting our innocence and promising Mrs Simpson that we would try to avoid prison in later life she decided it would be best if Jason was to be partnered with Mark and sit in the boat with her, she turned fast on her heels and proceeded to unceremoniously march the pair away, this surprised Mark so much that he started again to cry big fat tears and as he frenziedly gasped for breath he produced big bubbles of snot at the end of his un-punched nose, then without warning a small patch of urine appeared at the crotch of his trousers that proceeded effortlessly to spread the full length down his trousers and as he walked he became slower and more bow legged as each inch of his trousers absorbed the flow. Mrs Simpson wasn't overjoyed at this and for a second, I think she considered throwing Mark or Jason or both in the canal, after a few minutes inside the small canal side toilets World cup Willy emerged from the dressing rooms for the second, but not the last time that week.

My adult eyes felt heavy as I relaxed more than I had in a long time, nights when dreams had tossed and turned me forcing me back into consciousness melted, I was almost serene and memories of the gang bobbing and messing about on the water all those years ago kept me smiling, as our barge drifted easily through the water, everything felt right I was at ease with the world. The clipping of horse hooves beat like a joyous heart in cadenced rhythm with the water. I didn't mind being old, I just objected to feeling so tired.

The afternoon was calm, the breeze had given way to glorious sunshine, the august heat was enough to permeate the soul, Michaela looked beautiful in a white summer dress, and her expression too was easy as she drank in the sights. Llangollen ambled past in the far distance the shrill jangle of a steam train's whistle sounded as it trundled along with carriage windows down through the winding tracks, open fields surrounded by the splendour of the hills and valleys beyond, a new box of memories was made as we moved along the water we held hands and leaned against each other. I felt eleven again, I was happy and relaxed which is Llangollen's gift to its visitors.

We arrived mid-afternoon at Horseshoe Falls a beautiful weir that feeds the wonderful Llangollen Canal it is situated just west of Pontcysyllte Aqueduct which was our destination the following day. The falls is nowhere near as grand as the more famous Horseshoe Falls at Niagara but to me it is in every way superior, understated and peaceful the falls became a heritage site due to the feats of engineering it took to build the canal to its side and stunning opportunities it gives wildlife to flourish. If I was in God's own country I was now nestled in its heart.

I treasure Llangollen, its canal, wharf and falls as Michaela and I walked around the lock I remembered the gang and I being ushered away from the edge of the water by a lovely volunteer Mrs Betts, everyone wanted to be in her group, she was so kind and gentle with all of us and was a main stay of school trips having been on almost everyone with us since we started in the infants with her son Alex. We moved away and sat eating our prison infused lunches, Lee had is customary egg and cress, Jason Tuna that stunk like death but we couldn't move away or say anything because of his fondness for punching noses, Richard now recovered from his maladies and back in the fold munched happily with me on Peanut butter sandwiches Dan pretended his stick of rock was a cigar, his sandwiches ejected into the canal causing alarm, harassment and distress for the ducks who fled from them knowing them to be nuggets of pure evil. Dan watched the birds scatter as he lifted the sweet rock to his lips to take another impressive but wholly imaginary puff.

The simplest things back then made us happy, sat with our friends knowing nothing and fearing less, our families still complete and no understanding or exposure to sadness or loss. It is a unique and serene time in the ages of man that is wasted on youth. Feelings bought about by places and our memories of them are both delicate and transcendent for the soul if not incomprehensible for our brains to unravel and quite why the thoughts of a lunch time sandwich with friends sat on the grass by the water all those years ago resonated with me so much left me puzzled. It was a good time before life started throwing problems at us, we was content with stupid conversation and an unpunched nose.

Michaela and I sat in the same spot, as best as I could remember as me and the gang had done all those years before. My face looked back at me in the calm water, the last time I had seen my reflection here it had far less wrinkles and didn't have a worn appearance to it, my cheeky boy's face had made way for my slightly greying whiskers, my hair started a little further back than it once had. The years had in general been kind to me with only recent events being a real drain, for the first time I saw the resemblance I had to my mum and fooled myself for a second that her beautiful was looking back up at me.

My hair ruffled slightly in the breeze sending small delicate ripples across the water, I looked up across the falls to where the gang and I had played on the fallen trees, now long gone, replaced by new seedlings. Life had a funny way of moving you full circle. Llangollen was and is a special place, I thought to myself then that I will come back and visit it often, it is a place that allows me to pause, to think and just to sit and be. It is almost like time stands still here.

Life moves on, people change but somethings remain the same and as I headed towards the car, I sincerely hoped that this place would stay the same forever, this corner of wales was so idyllic and beautiful it was almost sinful to leave.

We made a quick detour across to Snowdonia and spend a pleasant couple of days exploring the villages that were scattered through the national park, the sights were out of this world the roads were a joy to drive on, A little after nine we were on the road headed towards Snowdonia with Llangollen and Shropshire behind us and pastures and with new and unexplored places ahead my childhood memories were refreshed and the smiling face of my eleven year old self stood shoulder to shoulder with my odd collection of friends in the rear mirror I felt glad that I had returned and that my road forward was so intrinsically to the road behind me, often travelled and worn a bit more battered than before but holding firm, the foundations laid solid enough to carry us all through. I understood then that you never have experiences and friends like the ones you have when you are eleven. I made a note to myself that I must call the gang back to together when I get home and treat them to a pint over stories of when we were very young. I decided one day I might even write a book about it!

The road west was a driver's paradise picturesque as freedom itself, long winding roads smooth as silk stretching as far as the eye could see as we wound through the hills and valleys large piles of slate scattered the fields shimmering in the sun looking almost alien as they radiated a cosmic glow. We made great time and within a few hours we were at the edge of the national park resplendent home of Harlech and Caernarfon Castles and Snowdonia itself. We decided to get our Barings stopping in the little village of Betws-Y-Coed carved to perfection by the River Conway, famous for its walking trails and equally its wonderful Cafes and restaurants we decided to dine out in the sunshine. We were blessed with another fine day the sun was warm on our backs and the breeze offered nothing more than a welcomed invitation to cool for a brief moment.

A local man, not too dissimilar to Albert Steptoe in looks but sporting a rather fine Rolex watch we met along the way overheard our debate and insisted we try the local cake shop specializing in welsh cakes of which he exulted their credentials describing them as fucking lovely bits of nosebag, famished and in need of coffee and sugar we had to find this coveted bastion of goodness, the cake shop did turn out to be an excellent little place if ever you find yourself in Betws-Y-Coed as we sat eating greedily Albert Steptoe passed by us on yet I suspect another money making errand glancing at us momentarily he exclaimed "fucking lovely isn't it?, more tea vicar!" To my absolute delight several ladies stuffing cake in their preverbal holes started to complain about his liberal application of the F word, choke and faint and protest in varying degrees of sincerity. Albert retorted back, "get over its ladies I'm sure you would rather be fucked than murdered". At this point I wanted nothing more than Albert to adopt me.

A day spent in the wonderful Snowdonia was in order, riding the train to the top of Snowdon admiring the views as the little train carried us towards the summit with the spirit of a pioneer the journey to the rooftop of wales capturing Snowden in all its beauty was exhilarating, I was equally thrilled to be there with Michaela, I realised that this was the first place that we had travelled to together that was new to us both, we was making fresh memories of our own, I felt hungry for adventure and to see everything our great country had to offer and what is more I had found the perfect person to do it with, sharing experiences and learning together understanding the world as much as we understood each other. I felt at peace and with a light heart and a twinkle in my eye the train arrived rolled in to take us back to base camp, I admired the many walkers that had opted to walk to the summit but it wasn't for me.

The following day after a fitful sleep was in the car as we continued west our destination was to be the most western point of Holyhead, after a few small diversions we arrived on the Isle of Anglesey taking time to explore the port side hills and grasslands, we trekked along the mountain side and took in the views of the lighthouse before we explored the pathways beyond eventually we stumbled upon an old abandoned house, odd in its design and complete with parapets and towers that appeared to go nowhere we decided to spend some time photographing the place, it became obvious to us after a while that it must have been a hotel at some point, it had closed many years before, the weeds and the trees had started to claim its edifice, a fire had sacked a large section on the western edge. As we walked its vast perimeter before descending back down towards the town, the daylight was starting to fade.

I wondered what had happened there and why the owners had left it to crumble, there was a slight air of tragedy about it. I made a few enquiries on my trusty phone and soon its story revealed itself. I was sad find out what fate had befallen it, it was obvious it burned down to then be left abandoned but I wondered if it had fallen foul of a wanton arsonist taken advantage of the remoteness and the loneliness of the place

The story goes that it, being a former mansion, then a hotel called Soldier's point. It was earmarked to be turned into a maritime museum when in the early hours of the morning it caught fire destroying much of its original features. It now stood as we found it, boarded and shuttered building looked sorry for itself.

As we drove back towards England, we made a few diversions as we criss-crossed the valleys giving Michaela the perfect opportunity to take photographs of the glorious views; slate glittered on the mountain as the sun hung low in the summer sky lighting it like a million candles, reflecting upwards towards the lit sky framing it beautifully. Holyhead Mountain sat behind us posing almost begging us to take its picture. The world seemed calm and well.

We arrived shortly in the small holiday resort of Treaddur where We found a fantastic little village shop selling anything you possibly need in life, it was crammed with everything from mouse traps to torches, we pushed the boat out and against my religion of being a bit of an orthodox tight arse splashed out five pence on a carrier bag (I thought when in Rome) and crammed it with as much food as we could fit without the handles exploding, soon we were off headed east making the long drive back to the English boarder. We was excited to be travelling through the night not stopping until we reached the boarder, in true Top Gear challenge style we cruised the roads back through wales along the A5 eating our crisps and sweets while happily listening to the radio.

Dusk gave way to a brilliant blue night sky, clear as mountain water the stars winked at me as they looked down, I had bought mum a star a few weeks previously like I had my uncle Brian years earlier, his star the "Norwegian Blue" the name given as a nod to the Monty Python parrot sketch sat twinkling with impish charm next to mum's "The Mumma" star.

I pondered the vast expanse of the universe as I gazed up, my place in it had always unsettled me but at that moment I felt sure that I should be exactly where I was. Everything felt right which was a feeling that had eluded me for a long time, nothing previously had seemed to fit, and the world was at odds with me. It had for a while seemed like a wild and lonely place but the two stars idly glistening in synchronicity as if having some wonderful unheard conversation made me smile and then for no reason cry.

As deep and misunderstood as the universe still is, I felt that the mind too as just as much a mystery, it's perhaps our greatest tool and the most misunderstood. From one moment to the next a mix of tiredness and emotion swept me up. I tried to neaten my mind, portioning feelings into different size bottles and boxes until I could no longer think straight. I was happy just being but yet I was riding waves of confusion that changed direction like the wind. Misdirection is a way that the mind protects itself from breaking and I was grateful that mine wasn't about to let me go mad although sometimes I felt that I would. In my darkest moments I knew all I had to do was look up at the stars until another wave arrived to soothe me.

Chapter Sixteen: Ironbridge and Iron Will

Jeremy Clarkson will attest that Isambard Kingdom Brunel is the greatest British person in history, a view that I tend to agree with, often heralded as the father of the industrial revolution his reach and contribution to this country is unparalleled and, in many ways, unsurpassed. After our late night and many miles of driving I awoke late but refreshed.

My gang and I had been on the coach for the short hop from Boreatton Park to the Iron Bridge gorge, we was all chatting excitedly in our groups, Jason and Daniel were holding court regaling us with stories of their made up adventures that we was happily drinking in rapaciously, the engine of our old coach rumbled along as we passed a small town there was a tiny little footbridge no more than 6 feet in length and three feet wide, upon seeing this little understated bridge the whole coach shouted "Ironbridge" in unison, how wrong we was.

When the real Iron Bridge honed into view it was a site to behold, I was instantly in love with the structure, the whole group was in silent awe of its standing, the River Severn hurried along in the gorge below. Built in 1781 from cast Iron, it is the poster boy and symbol of the industrial revolution. The gorge was formed during the last ice age and remained pretty much impassable for the next few thousand years until technology caught up enough to take on the challenge.

We walked across the bridge stopping mid-way to look down into the waters, we leaned against the high-pitched side rail, the trees swayed in mutual appreciation, We opened our little paper bags and set about our pork pies that we had bought form a little butcher's shop that claimed to have the best award winning pies in the land, excitedly we bit into them and just as quickly threw them to the waiting birds, they tasted like sadness.

Our snack ruined we crossed the bridge and had a look around a sweet little teddy bear shop where the prices were so incredibly high I assumed that the bears although beautiful must have been made from some rare and exotic materials like Queen Victoria's pubic hair or Arch duke Ferdinand's wig. Retreating we found some comfort in a little café overlooking the bridge, we had a fantastic tea and cake each, as we sat, I noticed several groups of school children sitting under the shade of the old sycamore trees painting and drawing the bridge, like mine years before their voices were chirpy and excited, they talked to each other in hushed but excited tones. They worked away happily. I hoped that they were making memories as good as the ones I made, life now for children I thought was far more complicated than it was for my generation, the internet had opened up the world far more quickly for them, they knew more but were no wiser. I didn't envy them their challenges, but I was hopeful that they would remember this place for the rest of their lives, I knew for certain that I would.

We headed to a small pottery museum just outside of Coalbrookdale, I remembered that me and my gang was not impressed by this, we was far to boyishly happy to appreciate a load of old bed pans and vases, Jason in a faux posh old lady's voice mimicked the tour guide as we lingered as far behind the main group as we could "some people like using these pots for, planting, some prefer them for cooking, for me though I like to use them for pissing" we fell about laughing drawing the ever watchful eye of our group leader, after a little chiding and some supressed laughter Mrs Betts let us continue on our way.

Looking back it seems very brave given our history that we should be allowed in a literal china shop, Miss Simpson aged tremendously in the few hours that we was at the pottery museum, it wasn't the coolest place for a bunch of eleven year old boys to be walking around, but we tried our best to stay out of trouble while heeding Miss Bett's story about the experiences of a particularly troubled bull in a china shop.

Michaela and I enjoyed ourselves very much, I sensed that in the thirty odd years that had passed since I was last here that I had matured just a little bit, I appreciated the craftmanship that went into making the little flowers that were still being sold at pocket money prices. I remembered back to my last visit, in the gift shop I had purchased one of these little flowers for mum, it had sat for years in her ornament case simple in design but stunning still. I resisted the temptation to buy another. I couldn't reason why I felt such an aversion to doing so but I felt almost superstitious about it.

We ventured onwards to Coalbrookdale to visit what remained of the Abraham derby blast furnaces, the whole area had developed during the industrial revolution and had been the home to the smelt ironworks that helped drive the industrial revolution making and supplying the much needed steam cylinders that powered the machines. Iron Bridge is credited as the heart of iron making industry but it the humble and unassuming village of Coalbrookdale just a few miles over that did the work, perhaps their most important commission is the gates for Hyde Park in London.

The iron museum made for a pleasant distraction, my interest was piqued by the the remains of the revolutionary water powered blast furnace and the Boy and Swan Fountain made for the great exhibition of 1851 alongside the Deerhound Table designed by sculptor John Bell for the Paris international exhibition of 1851. It was this point that I realized that I was perhaps turning into my mum. I had always been interested in all things industrial and machinery in general, I feared surrounded by piston engines and early examples of steam powered industrial might that my inner geek would explode releasing an ill-timed love piss down the front of my stunning trousers.

We browsed the giftshop and after speaking with my mortgage broker we bought a cast iron teapot and some casters that had been made from an original Brunel casting set which for the price of a small house in Nottingham now sits pride of place above the Aga in our kitchen. Before we could be tempted by some of the other wonderful items on display, we beat a hasty retreat.

The last thing on our list to do was to ride the old steam train in Telford, the gang and I had the pleasure of riding the steam train in Llangollen and we had the pleasure of riding along the Telford line, It was one of the last days before we headed home and the weather had begun to set in, the following day we was due to have one final go on the much coveted death slide which was called off due to the bad weather, instead we all forlornly traipsed around the small holding which had nowhere near the excitement of the death slide.

The gang and I arrived with the rest of our year in the carpark, horrible lunches in hand we lined up against the weather beaten station carpark wall, pissed about and got back into line again and after several time outs, My friend Lee who was still in a haze of adolescent ardor having spent the previous evening during hot chocolate time under a makeshift blanket doing Christ knows what with Julie Jones, whatever happened under that blanket he certainly liked it and wanted more of it but Julie was having none of it. Sick of being teased by us jealous nonparticipants he had finally snapped and while telling Debbie what she and principles could do and where they could go, was caught by Miss Betts mid-sentence during a stunning and imaginative foul mouthed rebuttal delaying our start to the station. Lined up and awaiting news of our fate we breathed a sigh of relieve when Miss Betts, who we all loved decided to give us all one more chance to behave, as if on cue Mark stopped crying adjusted his glasses just in time to receive a friendly tap on the nose from Jason, alas starting the line up again.

Michaela and I walked towards the platform I looked over to the wall that years earlier had been our stumbling ground, I smiled wryly as I arrived in the ticket hall, Springvale North was a lovely little station and the Telford Horsehay Steam Trust had done a great job with it. It felt not only authentic but lived in, preserved perfectly with sympathy and obvious love.

With our tickets in hand the train set off towards Lawley Village station, the day was cool and the steam hung in the air filling our noses as much as our hearts, I thought back to Jason and Adam both recreating a scene from the Youngs Ones TV show where one of the characters has his head knocked off while looking out of a train window, after Miss Betts had playfully dealt with the situation while stifling a laugh we settled down peering out of the nineteenth century glass windows at the rolling countryside.

This for me was my first "holiday", although we had schoolwork to do, I was having a wonderful time with my friends. At the start of the holiday we was all issued with an exercise book that was to be used as a holiday diary, not being known for my studious nature the teachers were taken back by the avid way that I wrote in mine, I was documenting the time of my life. It was at this point that I developed a liking for the written word, I was odd in many ways while my friends were listening to Five Star, Michael Jackson and the ilk I was listening to spoken word, devouring Tony Hancock, The Goons, Monty Python and the American classics such as Groucho Marx. I was blessed that I had friends that embraced my inner geek.

Words have always been important to me, they have the power to cause wars and deliver peace, they can move us to tears in one breathe and have us howling with laughter in the next. I poured my Eleven-year-old mind out in my diary not wanting to forget a second of this wonderful time. Looking back, I wish that I still had those books. When we were clearing out my mum's things in the months that followed her death, I hoped by some miracle that she had stored them away and they had perhaps survived, yet they remain lost.

The train soon pulled into Lawley Village, we decamped the train into glorious afternoon summer heat, having been led without incident to a small grassy patch we all sat down for our lunch, we all idly chatted as we ate the terrible food. Conversation was steered by our group leader Mrs Betts onto the subject of our highlight of the day, with a mouth full of sandwich Adam sprayed that his highlight was eating his lunch, Mrs Betts undeterred soldiered on and asked him other than food what was his highlight he replied having my drink, accepting defeat Mrs Betts turned to the girls that had spread themselves out making daisy chains and talking bollocks to each other, as she turned away I could swear that Mrs Betts mouthed fucking idiot to one of the other mums, in hindsight I had to agree with her.

After lunch we sent some time drawing pictures of the railway and filling out our activity sheets, I looked at some of the beautiful insignias on the trains the proud great western railway ran through the veins of this place, the trains stood their brilliant greens and blacks contrasting in perfect partnership. Beautifully restored with love and compassion the engines stood proudly anticipating our return journey if not a return to their glory days of full service.

Michaela sat where I had sat all those years before, her skin had started to catch the sun, slightly red faced but still beautiful I noticed that her hair had also turned a shade lighter and the blonde sparkled as she moved her head, it occurred to me then that she too needed this time away and that she was going on her own inner journey. I knew at that moment that I wanted her completely and utterly, it was the point when I knew that I loved her unconditionally.

Our picnic was a far less energetic affair than the last one I had here with the gang, there was no screams of pain from a punched nose or calls that someone had wet themselves, only the distant memory of everyone bundling on top of Michael Mateson to beat him up after he shouted "let's have a fight, everyone against me!" which we all thought was a marvelous idea, we was all enjoying ourselves fighting and shouting until the teachers and helpers all arrived to restore order, Jason delighted with his selection of uppercuts and body blows declared that it was alright that the fight had been ended as he had managed to get quite a good one into Michael's happy sacks, strangest of all was that Michael himself seemed to be pretty happy with the outcome. He was led away by the teachers breathless and holding his groin but still smiling his toothy smile as he gave us all the thumbs up, he still totally awesome to this day.

As we sat the easy sun lit the horizon casting shadows on everything it touched. We ate and drank at a leisurely pace our peace only interrupted by the occasional hissing and whistling of the waiting train that sat in the sidings.

Chapter Seventeen: Boaters and floaters

In the early morning haze, the brightly coloured canal boats cut through mist, the blues like Blue John gems stood out glowing with pride accompanying the ruby red and dappled gold paint. The craftsmanship of the boats was a thing of beauty, I didn't always see the beauty in the things that were obvious and right in front of my face, the beauty of crafted bridges, Ironwork on buildings and the wonder of feats of humble but brilliant engineering like the roof of St Pancreas railway station in London, all unique and works of genius and milestones marking the advancement of our achievements. Isambard Kingdom Brunel and his genius talent of design and engineering are well documented, but the art of his structures is often criminally overlooked.

We are blessed that in England alone we have twenty world heritage sites and English heritage itself has over four hundred historic buildings, monuments and outdoor spaces to look after, our rich Navel history has marked the banks of our rivers and the shores of our seas forever and the many fine organisations that help look after them for us should be both supported and admired.

The tragedy of the world wars is unmeasurable its scars plain to see, a chair at the table forever empty and the sadness of medical, scientific or human discoveries never coming to fruition as brilliant minds were lost, never able to fulfil their potential as they gave everything to the cause of world freedom and liberty. The loss to all nations was immense and my poor words will never be able to voice coherently the anguish that followed. The forts, Castles, bunkers and tunnels that still stand is a testament to our resilience, although functional they too are beautiful, they have stories of romance and redemption all of their own, they have human interest in spades that will not only surprise you but delight you. I was once advised that when whenever you walk through London make sure you look up as well as down because you will be amazed by the historic and important you will see, never has a truer word been said.

As much is also true about The Pontcysyllte Aqueduct built not as many think by Brunel but by Thomas Telford in 1805, the stream in the sky stands one hundred and twenty six feet at the middle allowing the River Dee to rush by underneath unhindered as it races towards Liverpool to the West, above the aqueduct carries my beloved Llangollen Canal, important and irresistible livewires crossing each other but like forbidden lovers never touching. From this stretch though the provision for horse drawn boats gives way to the powered variety moored just a short amble away down the steep banks.

We arrived as the mist was lifting in the early morning sun, eventually the Aqueduct itself made its presence known. At first the brick base rising from the water peered out through the mist and presently the arches at the top were resplendent as they crowned the horizon, a brightly painted red and green canal boat almost on cue floated gently along its top, its progress calm and measured unlike the unruly Dee running below. The song of the thrush in the aged trees and the call of the ducks below the canal made perfect contrast like a tale of two cities. Its beckoned Michaela and I forwards into its heart.

The top of the Aqueduct is not for the faint of heart and as I stood atop with the pose of a king I understood why we as children were not allowed to venture this far, The path was narrow with just enough space for a single file procession presenting some very shaky moments when someone came at you from the other side and with no protection against the canal water and a single railing to the side, both travellers approaching looking more and more nervous holding each other in their gaze, breath held tight to muster a few extra precious millimetres of space until exhaling with the joy of still being alive.

It was a risk I could see now that Mrs Simpson wasn't going to take especially given our track record. The reward for our efforts this time was though great, the river cut through the valley and the fields either side lined by beautiful trees and hedgerows as far as the eye could see, the grey roof tops of faraway houses dotted the hillsides, the slate shimmering in the rising sunlight almost blackened in appearance by the power of the sun reflecting through the water of the Dee below.

I drank in greedily the views the air was warm on my face and fresh in my lungs I stood unable to speak as the world in microcosm expanded below me. I was rueful that my classmates had missed the wondrous sight, but I reasoned that they would probably have been lost on us as children as we tried to throw each other into the water, over the edge or onto a barge bound for Liverpool. Either way in Mrs Simpson's eyes all would result in gruesome death and her professional pride dictated that she keep us all alive.

I remembered as I stood on the island at the top of the world the protests ringing out from the class when we was told that our expedition would not extend as far as the top where I now stood and we would instead be limited to the lower valley. I appreciated now the beauty of the lush green fields, the rush of the water and the myriad of wildlife that danced and ran through the very veins of the place as much part of its DNA as the water It was no consolation to us as children though and our relegation to the lower levels was something only now as an adult I could see as fair.

After several incidents of ignoramuses falling or being pushed into the water we all had served a time out on the banks of the river, we was all (except Jason who in frustration of a time out had punched Roy Kinnear's nose) allowed to head towards the skein of narrow boats, our task to draw one and copy the beautiful schematics that adorned them. When we arrived back into our classroom at school the following week we would use our drawings to design a sewing pattern that could be made into a table mat, I remembered our post-holiday project back a school fondly, there wasn't a SAT in sight.

Jason was soon released to the group on a warrant of good behaviour only to score a close own goal minutes later when he replied in earnest to a challenge from Mrs House to describe the canal boats and people bobbing along and living on the water, we all assumed that his answer "a bunch of gyppos roughing it in a caravan without wheels on the drink" wasn't the exact answer she was looking for, Elizabeth Welfare (the female Mark of the class) chimed in correctly with a far better and more politically correct answer we thought must have been right (but far too boring for me now to remember) as she was made bank monitor who would be in charge of grassing us all up if we stepped out of line any further, I could tell by the look on Jason's face that she would have to work hard for the rest of the day just to keep her nose un punched.

Later before bedding down that night Elizabeth's light summer jacket was by hand still unknown covered in large quantities of hot chocolate staining it beyond all recognition, Jason that night retired to his bed happy but for some reason very thirsty. To our delight Elizabeth's jacket when she wore it looked like it had succumbed to a massive explosion of diarrhoea to the bottom, Jason of course ensured everyone noticed it, like the hot chocolate his revenge was best served cold.

Soon after an underground chant in very hushed tones of why she was born so beautiful rescinded and feeling suitably repressed we settled to our craft. the sun was splendid and the worry of skin cancer, de-hydration and abduction had yet to be invented and left to our own devices on the river bank Jason soon got bored as was his style, he decided to venture onto one of the boats opening its creaky doors he disappeared inside, cat calling to us that we were all a bunch of blow outs and wankers, feeling that he had maybe gone a bit far this time the rest of the gang decided we would be better off to go and get on with some work elsewhere along the bank. We were all only too aware that when we returned to Boreatton Park later in the afternoon we would all be abseiling and riding the death wire slide that was to be the highlight of our holiday, the risk of losing this privilege was a gamble that was a hop, skip and a jump too far for this group of Thatcher's children, we had already lost our milk and we didn't want to lose anything else.

Very soon Mrs Simpson was explaining to the police that Jason was in fact not a genius cat burglar but a fucking idiot (my words not hers) and Looking back in hindsight I can now see why sometimes she looked a little misty eyed whenever the cane, cat or gallows were mentioned. In reality she had a tough job and gave up her time to take us on holiday receiving nothing extra in return.

Having avoided prison Jason was on house arrest and was sentenced to be no more than five inches from Mrs Simpson's side at any time, his dreams of abseiling and the death wire were now in tatters and further not helping himself Jason enquired about what the toilet arrangement would be, soon wishing that he had never asked and regretting his smart remark he paid his first visit to the girls toilets after much hysterical shrieking by the girls Jason red faced and finally beaten in spirit if not across the head and neck was relieved when he was finally confined to the coach with the poor driver for the rest of the afternoon. I don't think the driver ever really understood what he had done to deserve the punishment, but he seemed in quite a hurry to get us back to Boreatton Park, he had heard that one of the girls had a horrendous spell of diarrhoea that he really didn't want on his seats.

Michaela and I sat on the bank of the river our walk over the aqueduct and the climb across the steep banks on the other side had got our hunger up and a picnic of pork pies with egg running through it was most welcome as was the Scotch eggs, sausage rolls and sandwiches, we ate happily, the sky was almost blue with the exception of a white pillow of cloud that sat plumb and round in the centre of the sky, the sound of the water journeying towards the Mersey accompanied by the call of the wildlife was perfect.

It is often said that you should never go back to places that have captivated you in the past, they say it spoils the good memories but with a great a future ahead it felt difficult to forget the people I had met in my past. It felt right being here. I felt that I had connect with the people that linked me to my routes, some I had lost touch with along the way but I was delighted to recall the many that were still on the path with me connecting me evermore to where I came from. I felt safe, the rest of the journey would take me to places that I had never seen, places that mum and I always wanted to visit and had spoken about visiting, they all faced forward, and I was ready.

I felt sad in my own way thinking of all the wasted idol moments I had spent with mum when I could have been talking to her, finding out more about her childhood and her experiences instead of watching the television or talking nonsense (which we loved to do often) I wanted to understand the person as well as the lady that was my mum, I felt distant from her and this unsettled me, this is all a part of the grieving process I'm told but this was unlike anything I had felt before I felt a different type of sadness much heavier than feeling of loss or of missed opportunity, I was grieving for the things I hadn't said or done and here many miles from home with the lady of my dreams I made a promise to myself that I would ask the questions I wanted to ask without fear of feeling stupid, I would say out loud things I was thinking and more importantly feeling, I needed to make sure people knew I loved them and that I asked them all the things that I had been too reserved to ask before, on the banks of the river I was born again, not in some wanky way religion of any sort was not only out the window but had blown a mile down the road too, but in mind set it was that I felt ready. I was determined to be a better listener and to seize the opportunities before me to learn and grow. I was going to be me utterly and completely.

Some people that I had lost along the way I had a sudden need to re-connect with and as I sat eating a scotch egg it was decided in my mind that I wanted to see if I could re connect with some old friends that I had lost touch with over the years, there was no time like the present I felt a certain burden of guilt lift from my shoulders as I made mental notes to look into it as soon as I got home.

For now though Michaela was my willing accomplice as we had now well and truly run away from home, we could go where we wanted to see what and whom we wanted and for a second time I felt exhilarated and liberated by the prospect. The whole of the UK was spread before us and it was ours for the taking.

Chapter Eighteen: Maureen goes rogue

We were on the move, the countryside unfolded itself through the windows of the car revealing its beauty like a closeted secret, England was exceptionally beautiful in the morning light, the sweet-smelling grass met the clear blue sky in happy union. The sun was bold and bright, it hung proud in the mid-morning air. The few days of heaven in wales and the nostalgia of Llangollen behind us I was headed onto the M56 towards Saddleworth Moor, a place of such beauty that should never have been forced to keep such a dark secret.

It is beyond my comprehension that any human being could be so cruel to another human, to willingly take a life of another for whatever reason is alien to me and I doubt anyone on either side of the law could ever help me explain it. Saddleworth the scene of some of the worst and most evil child murders England and perhaps the world has ever seen. while it is itself indeed so very beautiful, stunningly so, with its rolling hills and still waters it is a veritable landscape painting, although it will be forever brushed with a subtle blue tone.

I remembered back to a few years ago, I was travelling back from Littlehampton in West Sussex to Royal Tonbridge Wells late one evening after a long day at work, my colleague and good friend Adrian Baker was with me as we crunched the miles along the A27 at of the hedgerow ran the smallest Rabbit, he darted straight under the wheel of my car, it was over in a second and there was nothing I could have done. Instantly without hesitation Adrian told me not to even think about it, I tried not to but the thought of something so small being there one moment and gone the next troubled me deeply, the fact that the course of my actions in a split second could have such dire significance to another living thing was overwhelming.

After a moment of silence I expressed my thoughts to my co-pilot, I confided in him that given how bad I felt about what had happened I couldn't imagine the grief that accidently killing someone by running them over accidentally, I don't know how I would function with the aftermath. As the miles rolled, we became quite the theologians, neither of us could comprehend how a member of the human race and society could have the capacity to deliberately harm another person let alone kill another. I won't name the moors killers, to do so would be a civil act and what they did is so far removed that we should erase them from society as there is no place for their kind. They opted out of their duty of self-governance that gives us the freedom to live with self-determination safely in our communities where our children can be safe policed with consent where the strongest in society will protect the weakest and most vulnerable; some call that Utopia whereas I call it common sense.

Pauline Reade, John Kilbride, Keith Bennett, Lesley Ann Downey and Edward Evans, each somebody's darling their names live on in the hearts of their community and in the spirit of resilience and dignity their families showed in the face of the most heinous and outrageous provocation, the innocent lives robbed of opportunities, hopes and dreams. Their small faces never to be seen at the dinner table again, a lifetime of Christmas presents unopened. The small peevish spots on the arse of humanity should be starved of the oxygen of publicity and notoriety they craved, insignificant examples, the very nadir of humanity.

Saddleworth was resplendent in the morning light, as we parked at the reservoir, families were out in abundance enjoying their afternoon, kites flew, dogs barked as children shrieked in unison. I was glad the sadness of the place had been triumphed laughter was everywhere. We soon found our Bearings and headed up the steep bank towards the water, it was flat deep and still. We headed east along the reservoir path determined to cover the entire two-and-a-half-mile trek around the Dovestone reservoir, in fine fettle we walked hand in hand and talked about everything and nothing. I was pleased to be in Michaela's company she looked beautiful in her buttercup summer dress, it flowed in the wind. We soon happened upon a much welcome ice cream van, with ice creams almost as big as our faces we strolled on. There is nothing like an ice cream to compliment a day out.

As I fell upon the vanilla goodness I was taken back to the beach at Broadstairs, it was the very early eighties and myself and my sister Cheryl were at the centre of one of the biggest ice cream incidents ever to happen that day, the repercussions I was sure would be felt as hard as they were during the Boughty Ferry ice cream van wars, I look back on it now as the great big ice cream incident.

Ice creams were a rare treat when we were kids but one thing that was guaranteed from a day at the beach was an ice cream and our excitement was as palpable as the excitement that a day at the beach had in store for us. I loved the beach as a small boy and nothing was better, this time there was extra excitement as soon as we were ready for the off, Mum told us we would be staying for the week with my Mum, Dad and grandparents in a chalet at the beach, had I have been slightly older I would have ejaculated there and then.

Our first day on the beach was uneventful, the sea was paddled and swam in, castles were built and destroyed with varying degrees of success followed by recriminations and war trials, mum ever fair laid down sanctions that both parties could work with, there followed only some minor boundary disputes and a short conflict which resulted in some long ranging unilateral disarmament. The day passed by swiftly it always did, after spending what seemed to us like several weeks of time trying to find the right spot on the beach, after much adult discussion a base camp would be set up sans a flag but the gaudiest windbreakers would soon fly in the wind, a shitty declaration that this land was our territorial claim, crappy and deadly deckchairs would then be precariously placed on the golden sand set to cause maximum injury to all users. It was then in a flash time to go home again and the broken chairs would ceremoniously be dumped into a bin along with sand laden sandwiches and assorted recovered treasures from the deep.

The Ice creams had been flowing pretty well thanks to Grandad George, generally beach huts selling ice cream to crazed children flanked by tired parents in the wild throws of heat stroke, sunburn and dehydration are not know to be the best value for money (thieving bastards) but this time we were blessed the two young girls serving in the little shack ladled the ice cream like the world was ending, ice cream poured down the cones onto our sticky hands, scores of children walked the beach with ice cream remnants run down their chests to their bellies, girls hair clumped with toffee sauce and not one spade handle was free from the three varieties of sauces that flowed like water into wine.

Giddy with excitement of our luck and toxic levels of sugar we achieved heaven in that small corner of Kent. On the fourth day suitably delirious from heatstroke and mad from thirst Grandad George took us for our now customary mountain of ice cream, the dream though was over. Gone were long queues as were the two girls. A tense standoff was taking place, a ferrety gentleman had innocently enquired as to the substantially reduce size of his little family of ferret's ice cream, in the girls place stood a man who must by reason of deduction been the very same Gino that the sign above the little shack boasted, engulfed in mania and mid tirade it was clear exactly how many shits he gave (not even three) and the amount of fucks both standard and flying (many many) he could care for about the portion control issues being experience by his customer.

As we stood nervously listening in it transpired that Gino being the owner had gone away for a few days for a funeral leaving his assistant in charge for the duration. During his absence however his assistant Maureen had fallen under the spell of what Gino described as a cockney cow gypsy scumbag from Sidcup. Head over heels in love and deliriously happy Maureen along with scumbag and his sister had decided to empty the till, the stock room and anything that didn't appear to be nailed down and load it into (to add insult to injury) Gino's own van and make off with the lot. To make matters worse before their departure they had spent three glorious days selling off all his ice cream at knock down prices pocketing all the cash leaving him with nothing, according to Maureen's mother who had been duly informed Maureen couldn't be reached as she had taken off all-inclusive to Mykonos for a period of time as yet unknown.

Michaela howled with laughter as I told her about Maureen and the Ice cream incident. It was nice to be able to enjoy the moors, we walked across the northern end amongst the Cottongrass, heather and crowberry that grew abundantly at every opportunity. The native birds screamed and darted overhead has we traversed the narrow pathways.

We made good time and made the 4 mile round walk in a little under a few hours, hot and thirsty we headed East to find somewhere to eat and drink eventually finding a small teashop on the outer reaches of the park where we managed to find the world's worse cup of tea which having gone cold left us even thirstier. Feeling teased we took the road north east and found some services, with some machine mixed coffee and the world's most expensive sandwiches.

For most of my career I have spent a lot of time on the road and although I have now become immune to the terrible food on offer at the over inflated prices, I have learnt to ignore it and carry on hungry but with the lack of a decent lunch and no news on when my dinner might be we decided to put our hotel for the night into our sights. The open air and walk had done me good, I reflected that I was warm and safe and that for too many is a not only a blessing but their biggest simple wish.

Chapter Nineteen: It's going down

After a great and well-earned evening meal and a fantastic sleep I took a final look around the hotel room I made sure that we had packed everything, Michaela in another beautiful summer dress was outside packing the car. The hotel room now looked bare as if we hadn't been there at all. It was now as clinical as we had found it Michaela having worked her magic not wishing to leave a mess or trace for the cleaners, her crime scene training with the Met Police was all too evident. I thought back to the day we had to return home on our school trip, the mixture of sadness and elation of seeing our families tossed in our heads.

As I stared at the white canvas of the wall I reflected on the time my friends had spent here and I longed for them, I wanted desperately to travel back to the eighties and see them all as we rushed to get our cases packed for the journey home. I was looking forward to seeing mum and my sisters again but couldn't help but feel that something was over, in a few weeks we would finish primary school and all the friends I had known for the last seven years were all to go our own ways although we would remain friends the compass was shifting.

The playground when we are small, like the street we live in becomes our world, friendships are formed and broken, love is won and lost and the laws of the playground followed these undeniable facts with the religious furore of a tabernacle band leader banging his drum so hard his watch flies off never to be seen again.

I recalled in my haze the day a dog run into the playground and was chased by three hundred self-qualified dog experts (that is until it turned nasty and saw the retreat of three hundred dog experts) I recalled the day Daniel Humphries was sent home for bringing in a pair of X Ray specs (they never did work and he never did see Ruth Brat's pants). I smiled at the memory of Lee getting caught trying to look up Miss Lewis' skirt (achieving nothing but a right hook). The games of marbles played on drain covers and the shrill sound of the girls singing skipping songs interrupted as Jason Tate ran through their lines in wanton destruction, they were simple happy technology free times.

The magnificence of the stupidity that reined over us and without internet or the inclination to ask things we were prepared to believe made me smile ruefully, I thought of the tale of the girl who ate the apple pip causing a tree to grow inside her, the one about bubble gum when swallowed staying inside you for seven long agonising years wrapping itself around eventually strangling your kidneys and the best one and to my mind, my favourite the one that ruefully warns that we shouldn't listen to anything Alice Haywood said because she had one tit bigger than the other.

The ridiculous rumours that circulated the school involving various people sitting on the laps of various relatives giving them all sorts of erections and peculiar dysfunctions, I remembered fondly the boy who ejaculated (purple sperm no less) into a swimming pool getting three girls pregnant and the one that Tim's oldest sister was really his mum, this bought about by way of payback for his valiant but failed attempted to convince the school that his real and full name was Tim "chop Suey" Churette forever marring him by way of explanation for his terrible proposition that not only was his sister really his mum but he had also the misfortune to have been hit on the head by a falling breeze block as a baby while his sister rocked him to sleep placing her for life in a mental institution (which was evidently more plausible than the name) all nonsense of course but nonsense that none the less passed into law because it was just so much fun.

We had our own self diagnosed maladies involving exploding colons bought about by deadly combinations of mint sweets and cola drinks, and the deadly disease that caused your poo to turn black and could only be cured by a thorough washing of the hands and the eating of raisins. I smiled fondly as I recalled the claptrap we believed which belonged only to the innocent from an age where anything no matter how stupid was abundant with the gift of the possible and in a google free world the boldest of the storytellers would be king.

Not long after mum died I started to develop a funny thing about new places, for the first few months I had a real sadness about travelling anywhere mum hadn't been, strange though it sounds even to my own ears I didn't want to go anywhere that she hadn't, I was walking through Stratford City in London while carrying out some piece of work or another one afternoon. The shopping centre had not long opened as part of the London Olympic stadium complex and as I walked, I saw all the shops, cafes and bars offering almost anything the heart desired. The families walking happily through the shops enjoying each other's company as much as sights and sounds of this new and exciting place should have bought me a happy glow, but it didn't, and I couldn't place why.

Everywhere you looked Olympic flags flew everywhere, as I looked up at them fluttering lazily in the breeze I felt a pang of overwhelming sadness, I couldn't be sure at the time but I felt like I was letting my mum down in some way being somewhere that she couldn't, taking part in things that she herself would love but could no longer do. I felt like I had let her down, as if I was betraying her in some way.

I missed her uncontrollably and there in the street in the middle of London I began at first to gently sob, quietly to myself, then to my surprise great big round hot tears began to fall stinging my eyes and staining my cheeks, caught off guard and completely alone I was at a loss as to what to do I was rooted to the spot, frozen in time in a unbearable debilitating madness. The sky began to swim, and the floor and ceiling started to collide, I could no longer fathom which way was up or down, my stomach lurched, and I knew that I was about to lose my legs. Try as I might move, I screamed silently at myself to move, but I had no control.

I was surprised at my predicament as my brain had generally always enjoyed a harmonious and informally good relationship with my legs, my ability to move one foot in front of the other propelling myself along had only ever so slightly been hampered in the past by the odd invite to dine with lady alcohol and some of her sisters. When I did join them I could more often than not remain coherent enough to avoid falling backwards out of a window or through the gap of a train as meets a platform but here I was now in foreign territory and I knew I was in trouble.

My brain begged for oxygen and mercy as my heart pounded in my chest so hard I could feel my eyes pulsing in perfect rhythm, I gasped for sweet air but nothing but a sharp intake of breath followed, with my head now tingling all over I could no longer remember where I was, like a sparkler waved by a child on a cold and frosty bonfire night my vison fizzed and my ears popped. TIMBER! I was going down.

I have had the lights go out on me three times in my life including this upsetting and most recent episode that terrified me to my bones as I thought in all seriousness that I was having a heart attack, the first time I passed out however was a much funnier affair laced with just the smallest hint of irony, I was at the time a young television salesman and while extolling the virtues of the company's fifty step safety check on all used televisions while marvelling at its reliability to a perspective buyer I was sent flying by way of electric shock across the room from my faulty fifty point safety checked deceitful and hateful bastard of a TV. Eventually I came to rest a short distance across the room under a stack of blank VHS cassettes. Upon coming round having been dragged (I'm told at my own request out the back to the shame bin) I shouted that the telly that had attempted to murder me or commit GBH at the very least wouldn't be the exact model the lucky couple would be taking home tonight, like a failed TV gameshow host I admitted defeat having only showed them what they could have won.

The second time I was felled was an altogether more exciting affair, while regaling my colleagues (the lucky devils) with a story about my old friend Mick Chilcott when one Christmas he was speed walking towards the tills to start moving the thirty deep queue through the checkout process when he hit an old relic of the past and my old adversary the plastic bag, wrapping around the soles of his shoes, aided by perpetual motion and a bit of pixie dust he slid along the floor and landed in a beautiful heap behind the counter, suitably embarrassed in less than a split second he shot up into the air declaring a meeting needed to be had in regards to the safe storage of plastic bags, As I re-told the story I did the leaping up in the air bit not realising that I was now stood in my excitement and stupidity in the door way, being almost six foot three inches I had not much room to manoeuvre and mid leap my head connected with the door frame and tongue lolling out my head I hit the deck to enthusiastic but unaware applause from my audience not realising that I had indeed just knocked a shade of shit out of myself, it was a case of goodnight Vienna.

I was now though in the most unfunny of circumstances, as my vision returned, I was greeted by the smiling face of the London ambulance service and several Olympic helpers that had seen me crash to the floor. I felt awful and was told that I had what they thought was a panic attack, my first and I'm glad to say my last.

Missing mum and overcome by feelings of grief and anger my brain had finally called a time out. Exhausted I sat on the pavement with the world passing by me. When you lose someone, you do a lot of thinking, introspection becomes your best friend. The shame is it's not a super cool type of best friend you know the one that turns up to your work on a boring Tuesday morning with a massive coffee for you and a plan to rob a bank, it's not even the type of friend that turns up at 7pm on a Friday night to take you out clubbing to cheer you up after you just found out your girlfriend isn't a girl. Introspection is the sort of best friend that will question whether the wet patch on the front of your trousers is urine, it's the friend that turns up to your house with a runny nose and raging cough to borrow £20 promptly infecting everyone then buggers off in your car. In short introspection is a pain in the arse that needs to piss off out the way so that you can talk to someone with a bit of authority.

Driving myself mad was a frequent hobby, I could easily fixate on some small detail of insignificance for hours or days on end, as much as I tried, I couldn't shake these fixated doubts that plagued me. We all react differently when we experience trauma, some people take on symptoms of illness, others go off the rails, I became quietly, but passionately obsessed with the corners of my picture frames becoming or being damaged. I once ordered a picture frame from some poor bastard on the internet, it duly arrived and to my horror when I opened the little parcel the corner was completely crushed, I was mortified. I raced onto the website to tell the seller that my world had ended. In blind panic I couldn't focus correctly to the point where I couldn't see the order for the frame among the list of other people's unwanted shit that I had bought. In my haste I hadn't also taken any pictures to send the seller. Feeling ever more shattered by the unfairness of it all I sat on the floor in the middle of the room and cried, not just a little but wailing great sobs.

I learned it's alright to be upset and sit in the darkness, but it's not OK to unpack and stay there too long. After a few minutes I managed to pull myself together and calmed myself down. I wondered over and over if anyone had ever seen such cruelty to an orphan. My thoughts gathered and spurred on by a copious amount of tea I soon messaged the seller, attaching the correct photos to a coherent message worthy of a United Nations plea bargain. My problems though were now just starting, what followed was a night of horror, constantly checking my phone every three minutes for a message telling me that everything will be OK and that the full might of Eddie Stobart's fleet supported by a small private army of civil engineers had been mobilized in order to deliver me a replacement picture frame, after all there was five pounds plus delivery at stake here. Why won't he answer me a little voice whispered in my head over and over until the small hours gave way to sunlight, after precious little sleep I awoke and leaped for my phone, to my relief and joy dav1123 had replied, a new frame was on its way and order had been restored to the universe.

A slight irritation to many had become a big deal for me, I knew my response wasn't proportionate, it was my way of deflecting my inner conflict, and it was my way of maintaining control. I found talking through my worries with my friends, no matter how incredulous they may have seemed worked, Introspection soon stopped being my friend, I made a conscious decision that no matter how embarrassing my fears were I would voice them, I had nothing to lose and my true friends would be embarrassed with me, not for me soon introspection got bored and it stopped coming around after a while and soon I was able to connect back with my real friends. The isolation you feel when you lose someone is huge, even when surrounded by people the propensity to feel lonely is acute. The desire to talk to someone about how you are feeling is fleeting, in one moment you want nothing but silence then in the next you just want to tell someone how unfair things are. The key thing to remember when someone is grieving, I think is to do nothing more than be there, to offer an ear and listen, to be patient and to have a hand ready to hold. The pain and anger will fade, tears will come and go but your person will come back to you as fast as they can.

Chapter Twenty: Sleepless Owl

The night can be a comfort or a curse, I remembered back to my school days at Tubbenden there was a book fair that the gang and I went to with much excitement, as we headed into the main hall our disappointment was palpable as we discovered to our horror a room full of books and not one ride to be seen. We was crestfallen to discover that there was multiple meaning to the word fair, and we decided that things were most unfair, as at the time I had not much interest in books and after the let-down that was a fair for books and not rides I was even less enamoured.

Begrudgingly and after some time spent reflecting on a future prison at Mrs Simpson's request we all trudged sadly around the hall, the smell of the books and the thousands of adventures that awaited us in their pages was completely lost on us bunch of bogey faced seven year olds.

One book though garnered much attention from us as it engaged our silly funny bones, if not our brains. Plop the owl that was afraid of the dark lay there upon a table like a veritable stream of bat piss in so much that it shone out while all else around us was dark. " Plop is Poo!" shouted Jason , who at this time was still developing his fondness for punching noses, so we all thought we better laugh at the not so subtle link as he joined the dots for our new friend Andrew who was a little bit daft. It was vital we felt that Andrew should be caught up quickly as Jason had punched a few noses so far and he was looking almost twitchy. So, it was now critical that he understood the connection between the owl in the book and shit.

After a short while browsing we was called together in our class groups and to a reaction of great apathy from the gang we were told that we would all be allowed a book each to take home to the value of 85P, the stars aligned for us that day as we all tittered at the thought that we would each be taking plop home in a little brown bag.

The book itself is one that I still have on my shelf in my office; it is one of a few books that I have kept with me through the years that still even now delights me, the house that sailed away being another favourite. Plop follows the trials of an Owl who is afraid of the dark and his mum sends him out into the world to explore his fears and along the way he meets different people and animals that all have their own unique reasons for loving the dark, the stand out moment in the book which I now for me holds so much more relevance to me.

Plop happens across an old lady sitting in the dark, soon he understands that the lady loves the dark for many reasons most importantly to her it means she can pretend she is still young and that her husband is still alive, in the dark she is no longer old and her small flat is no longer her prison cell, she goes on adventures whenever and wherever she wants. No longer limited by the grind of daily life or the harsh light of reality she is given peace and adventure in whatever measure she wishes. The lady teaches Plop to be bold and think outside his limits and welcome the darkness as an adventure to be grabbed.

Thinking back to the end of Mum's life I like to imagine that she had the same comfort in the still of night, when everyone had stopped fussing and she could sit and reflect she could be anyone she wanted to be and do anything she wanted to do, having the serenity as she did to accept what she couldn't change all the time having the courage to accept what was happening. In every way a remarkable lady that I still strive to live up to everyday.

I can't help but draw comparisons between myself now, here I was laying in the dark, and I allowed myself a brief flight of fancy. Here in this reality mum was alive, not being sure if this was a healthy way to think, or a good road to travel I thought about the little owl and for a few precious moments my mum was on the end of phone, telling me about her day. She was tired from a busy day of shopping, had seen my sisters and spent time in the garden with everyone, the barbecue was amazing and all the kids had fun, she remarked as to how grown up they all were and what beauties the girls had grown into and how hansom and tall her teenage grandsons were, how she looked forward to seeing us all the following weekend as we made our way home for the summer holiday break, reality bit in to me deeply, like gout biting straight at the heart, the photograph remained. The sun shone, mum was among many happy, smiling baby faces. The photograph of my dreams faded like a ghost you can't see.

Startled at the vividness of my mind I was surprised to find myself laying in my hotel bed miles from home, in the still of the night with only the company of a little owl called Plop. I had slept well but I had woken with a start and for a reason that I couldn't fathom I felt a little unsettled.

My relationship with sleep has always been an interesting one, even as a child I would drive my mum to distraction with my incessant wondering around, calls for water and general lack of ambition to become a world class level sleeper, I had to face the facts early in life that my sleeping habits were never going to take me to the Olympics.

For Christmas 1983 I was given a Sony Walkman, this completely changed life for me, I was able to listen to stories on my cassettes at night and soon I was going to bed happy as a sand boy. With my shiny new Walkman I was given some tapes that started to open up new worlds to me, among my new hoard of treasured tapes was

Sherlock Holmes battling the hound of the Baskervilles, Dicken's seminal classic A Christmas Carol, Willo the Wisp and my beloved the owl that was afraid of the dark. I was in heaven. Transported every night away from my worries and the boredom while waiting for sleep to come.

Things started to go wrong and then went very wrong for my mum and dad and shortly after the Christmas holidays we moved from our family home in Farnborough Kent back to my Grandad's House in Orpington a few miles away, I was delighted at the prospect of being next door to Danny and up the road from Ben again, I was going home.

I didn't know then, but my parent's marriage was failing and soon things would come to an end for them. A chapter of my life that I don't remember in any great or little detail come to that. At the weekends I would diligently do as I was told by mum and walk from school with Lee and Jason to my Grandad's house where I was to stay until my grandad would walk me home on Sunday night after dinner, knowing the uptight boy I was mum was diverting me away from the increasing tensions at home and frightened I would be too caught up in the death throes of her marriage she steered me away from the eye of the storm.

Lying awake in my bed at night the volume of my parent's discussions would at times reach fever pitch as the drama played out in varying waves of misery and recriminations, penetrating the stillness of the night like a shock and awe operation. My headphones and the world they led me into kept me from the real world and I was glad.

My tapes soon were well worn and my Uncle John, who was and still is a kind and generous man soon delivered me a stack of new ones, much different to ones I had already among the great pile of tapes he gave me was the very best talent of British comedy I was mesmerised as my initiation into the world of Comedy began, Soon

I was hooked on the classics Fawlty Towers, The Goon Show among many entertained and captivated. On comedian for me though stood out for me, a great comedy actor called Tony Hancock. His exploits in the fictional town of East Cheam in his ground-breaking half hour sitcom saw me through some tough times, transported back to an England well and truly routed in the 1950's gave me much comfort. I remember clearly the reunion party and the missing page with fondness, even today I am still a huge if not obsessive fan of Tony Hancock and his writers Ray Galton and Alan Simpson. The evenings accompanied by Hancock and Co became easier and soon I fell into a neat pattern of sleep; it seemed my problems were all over.

I came home from playing with Danny and Ben one gloriously sunny Saturday afternoon in the middle of a hot august, mum was sat in the living room, which I found unusual as she normally exclusively inhabited the kitchen as I sat watching the TV periodically wiping surplus sweat from my brow worked up through numerous rounds of enemy attacks as the English (Danny and I) put paid to Hitler's (Ben) diabolical plan to take over our street, suitably defeated and with the street and indeed England safe it was time to have a break. I noticed mum studying me, after a while she said in her calm and even tone that Dad wouldn't be coming home, I asked her if he would be again, her face looked tense but soft, for my young brain's benefit she merely answered no and she moved to give me a long and heartfelt hug that made everything in an instant seem okay again, as I assured mum I was OK the cries of Hitler attacking the green at the end of the road shattered my calm, it was lucky I arrived when I did, Hitler had the allied forces in a headlock having escaped a full nelson as reinforcements arrived Danny stopped turning purple just in time to see Hitler take a spectacular yet unskilled and frankly dangerous windmill punch to the throat flooring Hitler and winding Ben simultaneously, The German army now in their place were rounded up to be executed by means of being thrown off the nearest wall, life was great again and freedom reigned supreme. To celebrate the three amigos headed to my house to watch Roger Ramjet.

That night mum, Cheryl, Beccy, Donna and I dined on fish and chips, a rare treat in those days and we sat happily eating our chips, as a new and different family dynamic took shape to the background sounds of Saturday night gameshows and light entertainment a new chapter for us was just around the corner. I never felt afraid when mum was around, her determined look and strong character was enough for all us. I knew then that things would never be the same, but they were better.

The soundtrack of the countryside gently ushered in the dawn chorus; light crept through the curtains and painted the carpet with light. I had made it through a rare sleepless night and without a Sony Walkman too!

Chapter Twenty-one: pushing on

We arrived in Derbyshire a little after eleven, I had wanted to see the Peak district for many years, when I was at school we once had a visitor who had grown up on dales and had bought it to life for us with his colourful tales of his boyhood, straight out of a just William book, his years there took him into adulthood which saw him become a ranger, protecting the valuable species that thanks to the people that care for it flourishes in the environment, eventually he became a police officer in the county serving the people and as well as the animals, when asked by Mrs Anning my infant school teacher whether he preferred people to the animals he gave an almost toothless wry smile as he affirmed no. He preferred the animals because whatever ill they did each other they did it because they knew no better and were honest about it, unlike some folk he had to deal with in his time as a police officer, he recounted the time he saw a female police officer for the first time and recalled the shame he felt at the treatment she received as he explained to us that times were different then.

I was surprised at how vivid this memory was to me now; I smiled with apprehension hoping his beloved dales would soon be mine too. I wanted for no reason I could think of to connect with this great man I met, although I could no longer remember his name, I could appreciate his life's work. I could smell the inside of the classroom as his words in my mind revealed themselves to me. He was different to the many god bothering visitors that would come on story time Tuesday to talk to us about the subject we was studying that week, it never ceased to amaze me as to how often any subject could be turned onto the subject of god. I often sat in the classroom on the mat in the reading area absolutely puzzled by stories of people washing other people's feet and running a bread and fish and chip shop that got overturned outside the church in the market, I think I may have missed the point, but I enjoyed the stories one the less.

This man though was special, I knew that straight away, he was by the time we met well into his advanced years, through my boyhood eyes he appeared to me to be about two hundred years old, his cheeky grin was infectious and I remember the whole class laughing with him, he shook and rattled each time he laughed, he told us that he had met and married a young lass from Kent while she was on holiday in his beloved peak district and followed her there, he cackled that his wife was his wife and the dales his mistress, much to the red faced embarrassment of Mrs Anning which only seem to delight our guest even more. Too soon our time with him was over the class sighed in unison, after we had all said our good byes Debbie one of the girls in the class asked if we could all draw him a picture, Mrs Anning agreed this would be a splendid idea.

After lunch we all walked down the hill to the school's nature reserve and with big sheets of paper and wax crayons we sat in a large circle, we each chose something in the grove to draw and we spent what seemed like many carefree hours drawing the wonders that surrounded us, The pictures were duly packed up and sent by means unknown to us to our wonderful mystery guest. I'd like to think the pictures did reach him and he appreciated them for a while and that he knew that he had made an impact on a bunch of five years olds, especially this one that still holds him in mind all these years later.

I recently went back to have a look around my old school, I was disappointed to see that all the old exterior huts were long gone, the grove was now a car park that served the extension of the school. I stood looking through the chain linked fence at the buildings, I knew them well like and old friend, the old metal framed windows had long gone and new plastic ones that didn't leak rainwater on to your work took their place. The flat roof was still home to hundreds of tennis and footballs that sat weather worn and redundant, at least that hadn't changed.

There is something quintessentially English about our national parks and waterways, I wished more people could get access to them and enjoy them, as English as a Routemaster bus, black cab or any number of bright red letter boxes and sadly diminishing numbers of beautiful phone boxes, these are all equal icons of England all I needed now was for a beefeater to get out of a cab and post letter to perfect the scene. The thought of a beefeater made me feel hungry our now customary breakfast of egg, bacon and sausages was now just a sad distant memory, We had left our hotel early to get a head start on the day, I regretted our decision the moment we walked into the diner in a small hamlet.

As we walked through the door every instinct I had told me run, we was greeted by a low lit, low mood run down hovel called Nan's pantry it looked like nan had long since conked out leaving what can only be described as the cast of Fraggle Rock in a Dickensian nightmare to oversee Nan's empire as she spun in her grave at a medium pace. The place smelled of what I hoped wasn't destined to be the lunch special, the air was filled with the promise of boiled underpants while the décor screamed attempt nothing without gloves. The menu wept in a quiet corner as toast gaily burned in the background mixing with the effluvium of the secret ingredient which I soon understood to be two parts bitterness and one-part disappointment.

After a fortnight a minion that had recently escaped from hell gimped over to us, underwhelmed with perhaps how her career was going and with all the promise of a fight in the car park after she grunted "yes" at us, I made excuses for her demeanour realising perhaps she was tired after her earlier long quest for fire, she then returned having been strategically shaved to resemble a human and taught to walk upright.

Overwhelmed and embarrassed by the effusive welcome we had received we decided to scale back our usually over the top breakfast, opting for a simple bacon sandwich which resulted in a mild breakdown from the team who had by now had their smoking and arguing interrupted by us meddlesome customers. Sans a smile the head member of the banana bunch beat her chest to signal her understanding while stopping just short of flinging shit at us munted off to the kitchen to defrost a few of the smallest slices of bacon she could find to be skilfully cremated by the cook who to be fair had only been raised from the dead moments earlier. After a brief moment the kitchen announced that they don't normally do bacon sandwiches, I was surprised by this, realising that I had made the mistake of ordering something off of the menu. After some grunting and much pointing, together we invented the bacon sandwich and as quick as a flash just under an hour later two closely resembled bacon sandwiches arrived, I felt a little spoilt as only one of the sandwiches had the wrong sauce in it.

Having forgotten to ask the kitchen to hold the hair on our order it was apparent that the bread had last been fresh when Nan baked it before her passing, this had to be the worse breakfast I had ever been presented with, more bush tucker trial than anything else we soon headed out the door hungry from our trip to the zoo. This in hindsight may have been a tad unkind on my part but the food was terrible, and the service was awful. It was the first time that I refused to tuck in and get on with it.

Lunch was a much better affair, deep in the heart of the Peak district in the aptly named Hope Valley was a beautiful little place called the Samuel Fox, we had a lovely meal that we both fell on instantly, the trials of the day melted away as easily as the steak did. Much refreshed we were headed along the Monsal trail a beautiful walk carved out in nature with views across the national park, it felt like we were walking on the top of the world. There was stillness to the air interrupted only by the odd call and return of the sheep and cattle that scattered the hill tops.

We stayed the night in a beautiful little hotel on the dales, tired and sore we fell onto the bed. We had dined earlier on fantastic fish and chips while sat happily on the bonnet of our car on the moors completely alone we watched the stars above us contrasted against the deep dark almost purple sky, the night was warm and welcoming, in the distance Plop hooted his agreement. The world seemed alive with the possible. With the gift of a clear summer night I looked up to witness the birth of the universe and it didn't cost a penny. Tomorrow we would be going to Blue John Caves on the dales; I pondered the highs and lows and chuckled at the symmetry. Oscar Wilde was right some of us may be down in the gutter, but we can still look at the stars.

We arrived in Castleton arriving at the caves under the escort of beautiful sunshine, we almost missed the car park as it stood cut into the hills, the tiny little ticket office and shop stood proudly to welcome us, quiet and unassuming I liked this place from the off, it was in keeping with the beautiful village a few miles away, it was un tourist like and subtle.

The cavern itself cut into the limestone that was formed when millions of years ago it was formed from the deposits found on floor of the long receded great ocean, this can be evidenced as you walk through the caves by the sight of the many fossils that remain. Blue John, the mineral was first discovered almost two thousand years ago by the romans, it is a rare and strikingly beautiful mineral that to date has only been found in Castleton.

Rare items made of blue John have been found on excavation sights all over the world with two complete vases having been found as far away as ancient Pompei. It to this day hand mined as it's delicate make up makes the use of machinery or blasting impossible as it would destroy the complex structure of the stones themselves.

We walked through each of the caverns taking in the wonders, I felt small here. Millions of years of evolution stood before us, Michaela as always was able to take some stunning photographs getting the balance of light on the exposure just right. A small waterfall cascaded down from the top of the cave running into a small stream that run through the caves, the air was cool in contrast to the muggy August air above us. In contrast to the caves in Cheddar these seemed understated by comparison, I leaned my forehead on the chiselled wall of the cavern, it felt cool against my skin. We was almost entirely alone which for us was exciting, I pondered not for the first time my place in the universe. If the stalactites could hold on and keep going for millions of years, I felt sure that I too could remain on my path.

Chapter Twenty-two: The mum in the mirror

Running away for me was the only option, I needed space to put my thoughts into perspective and to try and understand myself a bit more. My time on the road with Michela was a real experience and it will stay with me for the rest of my life. I had some home truths about myself to deal with as I had learnt so much about myself, My sometimes caustic exterior was just how I kept myself protected, I used humour as a defence mechanism my laughter in reality a silent scream begging the room not to hurt me. I desperately wanted to impress people and show them I'm not stupid by publically correcting others when they faltered. All these things I have decided to work on, the path is long, but I'm determined to try and be every bit as fantastic my mum was, I will live to her principles and values. It is a very high bar I have set myself but I will try to make my mum proud of me and become the man she taught me to be, too much nonsense got in my way and I lost direction, with time and the space to reflect on my life and I started making the much needed changes.

My reflection bothers me, I can't help that. It always has but I now understand that my body is the greatest thing I will ever possess, When I ask it to put one foot in front of the other it responds and my body follows, My mind can recall all the wonderful times I have with my family and friends, It recalls the gang at school and allows me to think, feel and love. There is no greater reason to love what I have to work with than that.

So many people affected by cruel diseases that steal mums and dads, memories and movement that slowly creeps up like a ghoul not always killing them quickly with civil dignity but still taking their lives in other twisted and terrible ways. I celebrate what I have every day, I will never again let anyone tell me what I have isn't perfect. I feel, I think, and I breathe. I have plenty and that will do.

I learned not to be afraid of labels, you are not what others perceive you to be, a label is exactly that. Just a handy marker for convenience. A blue sheet can be a throw and a sheet, it is a blue sheet that is the label we put upon it but if you spread it over the back of your sofa it easily becomes a throw, the packet label though is for a blue sheet and that will never change, its use and worth however can't be measured merely because it is blue (fact) and a sheet (fact), it may be a child's best friend or comforter but to a stranger on a train looking in it may merely be a rag but to the little boy or girl it is their absolute comfort and their access at night to calming sleep or the freedom of pain after a fall, to the parent it is a god send, its fibres more valuable than spun gold. The label doesn't matter. The purpose is everything. Make sure despite your labels you know your purpose.

I have given up trying to shake the labels that other people want to place on me; I'm not frightened of them anymore. I used to be, I would walk into a room worried about what people would think and how they would react to me, the laughing behind my back that used to fill me with cold dread no longer haunts me the honest truth is I will never shake the labels of others. I choose now not to spend that energy. It took me a long time to understand the concept that no opinion is wrong, no matter how outrageous or insidious it is, however the facts people base their opinions on are quite often wrong, the brain can often confuse opinion for fact, I choose now how I engage with people who are caught up in their own pseudo reality that just aren't ready to listen.

How we choose to tackle ignorance, bigotry and unkindness is down to our own sensibilities. In a world of keyboard warriors correcting the minute grammar and spelling for people who never asked to be corrected is just plain rude, it shows a real lack of emotional intelligence on the part of the self-appointed teacher, I cringe when a person pounces on another correcting a minor brain fart when the wrong word is used, intelligent and educated people allow the error to slip quietly past knowing what was meant and allow the other person to feel valued and wanted and air their view. This is the mind-set of the true intellectual, they understand although the spelling and grammar may not be right, the point made is valid and they gain knowledge that the grammar and spelling police would long have shut down.

Appearances are deceptive; Hollywood in its infancy had many challenges and through adversity comes innovation. The lack of sound meant a gift for visual storytelling was king, Stan laurel, Charlie Chaplin, Buster Keyton and Harold Lloyd all geniuses of their craft and pioneers of the silver screen adopted a style for the screen that the villain of the piece would be depicted by a fat man with a top hat and a deep dark moustache with a fat overbearing woman in tow. The fool would be poorly dressed or again fat and slow. Go back a few short years before to Victorian Britain and perceptions would have been very different it was desirable to be fat as it was a sign of wealth and prosperity, and you would be granted access to plenty of fine fanny by gaslight as much as one would have desired "you are looking really fucking fat Dave, well done mate" "yes" came the reply "I can't complain I've had a good month down at the old match factory, if the good luck continues and things continue the way they are I may be obese by the end of the year, fingers crossed".

Cinema though conditioned us to think fat was bad and stupid, it's a lazy stereotype that I can't change but I don't have to buy into it. People are not fat; they have fat it doesn't define them it is not who they are. I now understand that no one is as fat as they imagine and I would rather listen to Albert Einstein dressed as a clown than Adolf Hitler in a suit, In a world so pre-occupied with the size and colour of the wrapper they bypass the sweet inside and miss out on all its goodness and everything that it has to offer. If you don't like the look of a sweet, we move on past it, we leave it alone we don't prod and damage it.

It's sad that sometimes we have the capacity to treat a sweets and biscuits better than a person, just like the sweets it is perfectly possible to leave the person alone and move on, pass them over with a polite sorry not for me, not interested. If they ask you out on date be flattered you don't have to accept but don't damage someone just because they aren't for you, I guarantee someone will come along that will want them, I'm living proof of that, The journey for me was a long one and like the orange quality street I was in the tin for a long time. How we treat others is a true reflection of how we really see ourselves the uglier the behaviour towards others is perhaps a sign of how we feel, it is far easier to vent our pent up frustration about ourselves and direct it towards other people than deal with what we don't like about ourselves in the first place.

Life even when you are surrounded by people can be a lonely and scary place, it isn't always understood that it is OK not to be OK and we all have the capacity to get ourselves into a mess from time to time. True strength comes from asking for help or screaming for the world to stop because you want to get off; our vulnerability is what makes us human. Although life has become easier in many ways social media has opened up new worlds of possible to us, Facebook is full of people having fantastic holidays, driving exotic cars and living in beach front houses as endless photographs of smiling veneered toothed models live their best life as we sit in a two up two down house in the pissing rain.

Unattainable airbrushed bodies and impossible wealth seems to be everywhere, and the money seems to run as freely as the champagne, it's not real. It didn't exist before Facebook and it doesn't exist when the cameras go away. If you have food in your belly and the lights are on above you, then you are successful. Your worth is not measured by the amount you earn or the job you do, most of the decisions you make as you go through life are half chance anyway and whether you believe you can or whether you believe you can't you are absolutely right.

People rarely remember what you said or what you bought them, but they will remember how you made them feel, be careful with other people's feelings and patient with those that offer you their help and advice. Don't think about ways your partner makes you happy, think about ways you can make them happy, in turn they will reciprocate and things I promise really will be OK. Life will come to beat you down, you can't get off this planet alive and a little of what you love or fancy won't hurt, surround yourself with people that love you enough to challenge you constructively to help you grow. Be wary of people that smile when you fail, don't let anyone count the times you fall, celebrate with the ones that count the times you get back up, dust you down and help you move on, people that are negative towards you, your hopes and your aspirations are scared of losing you, they hold you back in fear you will outgrow them and leave, if they have that much of a low opinion of you in the first place they don't have a right to be in your life and they aren't worth your time anyway.

Lastly I realised people are precious, take loads of photos, send cards and write something nice about someone on Facebook for no reason at all, tell them their looks great, there crappy car is awesome, tell them the cake they backed looks delicious, be their champion. Be the cheerleader, you never know your kind words just might be the critical difference to someone. I have been hurt many times by careless words of strangers or indeed by friends. We have all been hurt by ex-partners and I'm sure I have people equally whether I meant to or not, we can all be thoughtless at times. If your boyfriend or girlfriend speaks about an ex too often be gentle with them they don't constantly talk about them because they are not over them, they talk about them because they aren't over what they did to them, help them through it, be calm and let them talk. You can't fix anyone but the one thing I do know is you can hold their hand along the way while they fix themselves.

As I reflected on what I had learnt about myself I realised that some of it wasn't pretty and when I was honest with myself it was tough to comprehend, as I looked at the list of things written on the page the harsh black and white stared back at me in mutual loathing, we hated each other. Like Ebenezer Scrooge but without the ghosts and a beautiful Victorian setting I was relieved of the guilt and the noise that I carried, it wasn't too late for me to change. I never once heard my mum speak ill of anyone, she never spoke behind her friends backs and she always made sure people felt welcomed and special, if our friends were in tears she would hug them as if they were her own, she was known by all of my sister's and my own friends as the Mumma, entirely selfless and a lady of the highest principles. I was now free to be the person I wanted to be, I could hold myself to values my mum held and be just as good a person or at least the best version of myself and the solution was simple. I just had to stop being an arsehole and one thing the world needs less of is arseholes.

Chapter Twenty-three: Old world, new money

We travelled east through Derbyshire stopping at beautiful place after beautiful place eventually arriving at a designated area of outstanding natural beauty, which after a long drive in the car thankfully had a toilet. I paused to wonder why we would ever need these things designated, I felt with some confidence I could work these things out myself, having got myself this far I felt able to avoid any wasted time stood behind the back of a Pound shop marvelling at their bins. Although I think it would be quicker to have all their stock delivered straight to the bin to save us putting things we have bought there in the bin ourselves two minutes after we got them home, I smiled as visions of Reggie Perrin and his grot shops created by the wonderful David Nobbs, the voice of CJ, Reggie's boss declaring "I didn't get where I am today by not putting pound shop purchases straight in the bin". I forgave myself a slight chuckle that developed into a cough as I realised the gentleman standing next to me may think I was laughing at his penis. He already looked flustered as he wrestled with a shy bladder or to keep a fart in. I made a mental note to myself that I really should concentrate when I'm having a wee in a public toilet.

I felt a slight melancholy now, I seemed to have so much more in common with poor old Reggie in the past, now I was feeling much better and the time away from things was having the desired effect on me. I now couldn't imagine myself like Reggie walking into the sea in an attempt to eradicate himself from history and walk away from his life so completely. The temptation for me was fleeting.

When mum died the immediate pain was torment, I could quite easily have jumped off the ferry that night but something inside me a kind of self-preservation kicked in. Time doesn't teach you how to cope with loss it, it helps you deal with it, live with it and as much as I would change the polarity of the earth to change things, I realised I couldn't.

We all find ways to cope, to release the pressure. Being vulnerable is OK, we all have different capacities to deal with pain, some behaviours are learned, when a child is hurt either emotionally or physically our first instinct is to tell them not to cry and to come on or cheer up. From an incredibly young age society inadvertently puts restrictions on us, I am guilty as the next person of conforming to these social constraints myself, and we need to make sure that people understand it's OK not to be OK sometimes, feelings are real and our strength will come from the next generation of children understanding that emotional resilience and good mental wellbeing are As important as any academic achievement.

If in just one generation, children can be radicalised into social hatred, we can by that measure in one generation teach tolerance, kindness and good mental health awareness in our schools, maybe go one step further and teach children to relax, to meditate and listen to their bodies then maybe in time they will understand themselves better and the differences they have with others can be celebrated. Those that do well in terms of academic achievement will no doubt still go on to be doctors, lawyers and politicians. They will then have the ability to make decisions that affect the lives of the less fortunate, they can assist the teams of good Samaritans, social workers and volunteers that tirelessly work to help the disabled receive the social help and support they deserve, the children that can't fit whatever the reason in the main stream school system, the struggling teen who leaves our care system with no onward support and no prospect of achievement because the good people able and willing to help have their hand tied by the decisions of others in a position of power that tell us to have a stiff upper lip and take ourselves off to a darkened room so as not to be an embarrassment when we cry.

If we as society could achieve that then maybe we would have altruistically driven emotionally balanced leaders that could free the tied hands of the people on the ground to offer help and support, to look holistically at the issues and the causes of our problems taking real accountability and delivering solutions one person at a time. It's OK to cry and to be sad and to feel that you are losing your mind; it's not OK to say otherwise. We could live in a society that will strive to prevent things going wrong rather than expecting our police and ambulance services to patch up and pick up the mess often when it is too late. The police and NHS are not failing institutions, nor are our schools they are institutions that do the very best everyday driven by wonderful people that they themselves have been failed on many levels but still give their souls away to make the world a better place. It's time we stopped talking to the vulnerable and the disenfranchised and started listening to them.

The Derbyshire air had obviously cleared my mind as I had cleared my bladder. Driving onwards we stopped for an all-day breakfast in a little American themed diner that had become part of the roadside furniture. I was starving, and I couldn't wait to taste the Bacon and eggs that arrived impossibly quickly at our table. The early sun was already bright and hot, I felt that after some time of reflection I had made a little progress and more of the world made sense to me, I wasn't quite so muddled or confused.

The day was glorious I breathed in the liquid sunshine as Michaela and I walked along the banks of the river Wye, the ducks skimmed across the water in a serene Ballet the dramatic thrashing of their legs beneath the water hidden from view as they ducked and dived in unison, the water was clear and blue in stark contrast to the green of the hills behind it, it was like stepping back in time, our pace slowed as we crossed a small bridge pausing at the middle we gazed at the view endless possibility was stretched out before us.

An older couple stepped into view as they half marched, half stampeded along the footpath, the couple maybe in their seventies nodded a silent hello as they past us, I remembered that as a child mum and I would walk from our house to the local high street, thinking nothing of walking the four miles each way, which now for many could never be attempted without a car, an emergency supply kit and a selection of hard boiled sweets. It was funny how things changed in such a short space of time.

My mum on our trips to the shops would keep us entertained as we walked with classic games like eye spy and who can be quiet the longest (I suspect she may have stumbled upon this one on a particularly stressful sort of day). Things were different then and a lot of the things that mum used to say echoed around my head and Michaela was soon laughing at how we used to live. I recalled a time when I was well and truly caught in the semantics of the day.

Looking forward to two hardboiled strawberry lollies meanly drizzled in some type of mingy cooking chocolate from the local ice cream van, I had been busy moving the dirt and grime around the bonnet of my aunt Viv's car on the promise of a nice shiny ten pence piece, delirious at the prospect of the sugar and artificial colouring entering my system and sending me on a journey of full flavour behaviour I was cress fallen when she reached into her purse and produced not a shiny ten pence but a two pence piece, Viv was known for her avid and enthusiastic ways of obtaining, keeping and ultimately never spending money. Disappointed (where was Jason when you needed a nose punched) in temper I dashed the coin to the ground, a little hurt and surprised Viv remonstrated with me that this was the going rate and what we had agreed, to this day I think she skilfully duped me with the promise of a tuppence not ten pence, in a fit of juvenile denial I accused her of duplicitous dealings (or at least I screamed at her) "who says tuppence, what is a tuppence anyway", to me a tuppence was something my grandad told my teenage neighbour

Sarah up the road to keep her hand on when she went out with her boyfriend and had absolutely nothing to do with my cash transaction.

From that moment onwards I was alert to Viv and anyone else's coy and deceptive use of old money terms, I soon understood what half a bar, a bob and to Viv's dismay what a tuppence was, I was equally as baffled by telling of the time. In the tears before mobile phones, computers and even digital watches telling us the time along with when to eat, sleep and poop. My childhood brain struggled to understand that the big three on the clock was fifteen and the third hand was seconds baffled me, no wonder we all ended up a state.

 In a time before endless alarms go off in offices all over the land telling the water wankers when to have a drink. A guy in the office I used to share had a watch that will scold him if he has a biscuit without it telling him its's ok. It bleeps at him at 11am each morning "right you fat little fuck, you can have now have a biscuit as you walked up the stairs a week last Monday, you have one and one only, none of this one for each hand bullshit you pulled yesterday, now plug me in its been six minutes since you charged me. When you have done that you can drop and give me ten".

Growing up we would endlessly be on a quest to find a clock and then when our mission was accomplished we would spend an age trying to work out if it was right, staring endlessly at its face waiting for the minute hand to move just enough to tell us it was working, we as a nation spent most of the early eighties therefore five minutes late for everything, which was Ok because unless you were posh enough to have a watch then no one was any wiser, the unit of time back then required a degree in the dialects of old England, A simple it's eight thirty five back then would have to be translated from some archaic pre ramble, something like its five and twenty to nine, it was like a time tax on us children and the stupid.

For years we were convinced that there was only fifty minutes in an hour. Even if we took the five minutes off to see if the clock was working we was still owed another five minutes, we later worked out that we was set up always to arrive on time those five minutes proving a much needed buffer to get us anywhere on time. It was a simpler time when yet to be discovered technologies hadn't crept into our everyday life, when we were thirsty, we drank, we ate biscuits until they ran out or our parents caught us. A watch was a marvel if it could be running under water for more than five seconds and still work.

One afternoon at school our gang was caught up in a mania, that Christmas Casio had made the digital watch affordable for all and it was on every ones Christmas list, we all arrived back to school after the holidays to a new craze which required every ones watch to be tested to destruction, the craze kicked off quite innocently when Daniel arrived to school with a brand new spanking Casio with alarm function, it boasted a light and to be waterproof to a depth of five hundred metres. Soon things turned ugly as Lee felt his Casio that had a stop watch was now slighted and looking rather rural compared to the promise of Daniel's deep sea diving adventures and the world of possibilities that only the ability to tell the time in a semi-darken room could offer. Soon two camps were disorganising themselves in the boy's toilets. We had decided the most important thing was the water resistance of any time piece, everything else was just bollocks.

Michaela giggled as we walked back to the car having stretched our legs, relieved ourselves and taken in some large lung full of air, keen to know what watch indeed the superior, I had to admit that unfortunately we never found out as our underground watch fight club was raided after a tip off from what we was told was from a prefect, although stinky fingers to this day is still in the frame. We will never know what watch is best but that is OK because I know that tuppence is tuppence, and it now won't buy you a penny sweet.

Chapter Twenty-four: is there jam and custard still for tea?

Like Robin Hood I was soon to be riding through the glens of Nottinghamshire, Sherwood Forest awaited us. The Peak District national park had been a kind and generous host to us, and I was feeling quite sad to be leaving. It was in this beautiful part of the world that I decided that I wasn't tired of life, merely just London and I vowed to myself that I will make the change and become country gentlemen. We had stayed in Buxton the previous evening and had sampled perhaps the world's greatest fish and chips. We knew we were fish out of water (pardon the pun) when paying for our food, the smart looking lady behind the counter efficiently asked for ten pounds, I thought it was a little bit dear for a portion of fish and chips and handed over two crisp ten pound notes, puzzled the lady handed us one back saying "no its ten pounds altogether". Amazed that such great looking and generous portions could cost just five pounds I found myself explaining that we was indeed from London and things were rather dearer there, the owner looked at me wistfully as he considered the prospect that he could have been ripping the stupid townies off for years, he looked like he wanted to cry and beat his business advisor, we left him conflicted by what to do first as we searched for bench to sit on. We ate in a state of complete bliss and contentment overlooking moorland views in the bright sunshine and cool fresh evening air.

The following morning we made the short trip down to Bakewell from Buxton as we couldn't resist the gauntlet that a Comedy hero of mine Ade Edmundson had thrown down to try a Bakewell pudding and a tart in its birthplace and decide for ourselves which one was best, never had the inclusion of eggs in a recipe mattered so much to so many.

The history of the tart and the pudding are steeped in historic inaccuracies and much legend, it is as controversial as the debate New Zealand and Australia have over the humble Pavlova, much debate has gone into this subject and it is as divisive today as was then. I loved the passion and the boastful and plentiful signs adorning many establishments, some outright calling other competitors claims bullshit, it was fascinating, friendly and very tongue in cheek. I absolutely loved Bakewell, the beautiful and calming influence of the river Wye runs through the outskirts with a welcoming pub on its left bank surrounded by overweight panting swans and ducks that clumsily mooched in the water for the crusts of surplus Bakewell tart and puddings thrown to them by tourists trembling through the sugar rush and hyperglycaemic comas that only a genuine Bakewell pudding can offer. We was in luck as every single establishment in Bakewell laid claim to being the true birthplace of the pudding and the tart, to claim to be the inventor of both was a mere folly and was a boast too far for any self-respecting inventor of Pudding or tart and any such fool would be called out on their bullshit and dragged around the town on a small cart like device.

The village itself is a perfect complement to the national park beyond, it was a fine way to leave Derbyshire, we had travelled far and wide, and we had seen the best the peak district and Derbyshire had to offer. We had sailed in small boats on underground rivers and traversed its caves and walked its villages. The lakes, rivers and streams that cut their way through the Pennines were beautiful and tranquil, I felt at ease and calm. It has that effect on you and Bakewell was a perfect goodbye.

We parked the car and was soon headed to Mrs Wilson's old cottage which is one of the leading birthplaces of the Bakewell pudding, we soon passed a local convenience shop, feeling thirsty we popped in, there just inside the door stood the largest display of

Cherry Bakewell cakes they were made by a formal gentleman with an exceedingly good reputation for making cakes.

Our journey into sugar had begun in earnest, I grabbed a box of cakes and some with some refreshing cold drinks and as it was a nice day we decided to go posh in order to match the beautiful scenery suggested we should and bought glass bottles and feeling a little like Lord Fauntleroy I decided a box of cherry treats were in order to keep me going until we arrived the high street to begin our quest for cake.

As we stood in the queue to pay we felt the eyes upon us, several older ladies looked at our boxed perfections with disgust and I was certain that under hushed towns and muttered breath I was sure I was being labelled a typical cockney cow by a passing member of the local blue rinse brigade. We realised the full extent of how far reaching corporate hand was, stocking Bakewell on mass in the Bakewell branch of their operation seemed a solid proposition to me until it was our turn to pay, as we presented our wares the result of Flossie our server seeing our Bakewell tarts was equal in reaction to me climbing onto the counter producing the world's biggest shit and wiping my bum with the end of her nose while peeing into her lunchbox singing the tricolour.

Needless to say we soon found out she didn't agree with the stocking of such shit, it was almost with religious fervour that we discovered the wages of sin was boxed Bakewell shaped, before she could grab her tambourine and my testicles we escaped out into the gorgeous sunshine, clutching our devil sanctioned treats baked fresh in the ovens of hell we escaped, I was certain I heard someone shout "quick, they're getting away, to the cake car. Bakewell power!" but fortunately Flossie was side-tracked by some poor German bastard that had attempted to start another world war with his demands for directions and Stollen cake.

We sat watching the world go by from the village green and after a look round the craft market we flipped a coin and were headed to find the birthplace of the pudding first. The pudding shop was full to the brim of puddings, cakes, creams and everything little girls are made of. We order a pudding and a tart to share and sat in the little courtyard with strong but sweet coffees. I was in heaven, the views were stunning and the guilt of our earlier crimes against cake on the wane as we tucked in to our pudding, never had I wanted a tin a custard more in my life but with a trip to the local store now out of the question we finished our half and soon the tart was done, with just crumbs and remorse left I was determined to find custard and the birthplace of the now elusive tart in that order.

We sat eagerly awaiting the next round of tart and pudding; we sat this time in a beautiful tea garden, some children played while their parents relaxed and drank in their surroundings and took on large quantities of caffeine to get them through what was looking like by the excitement of the children a very long day. The illicit carton of custard in our bag was calling me like a siren to the sea, relieved that we wasn't subjected to a frisk by the cake police on entry I was glad I didn't have to smuggle the custard in and we could enjoy it safe in the knowledge it hadn't travelled in anyone's arse.

A little girl on the table next to us was about three years old and as cute as a button and the size of a dot. She arrived at the table just ahead of her dad who was weighed down with vast quantities of cakes and drinks. I watched them as they bit into their treats, The little girl I feared hadn't received the memo and as soon as she took her first bite of pudding spat it out and shrieked "this is shit!" at which point her mortified parents caught my eye as we all burst into laughter. It was one of those lovely communal moments that you remember long after the event. Unimpressed the girl took herself off to play as her parents soldiered on with pudding ruing their decision to stay local and not try the tart (which I was now learning was thought locally to be plebeian). Michaela agreed with me that we were tart people and I started to feel a little guilty that deep down I realised I still preferred the exceedingly good ones I have had earlier.

Soon we had finished our tart and tackled the pudding, as I reached into our bag a voice in a thick London accent from the table next to ours muttered in closeted tones "this needs custard" as if by magic I produced with split second timing my carton of Devon goodness, the owner of the voice regarded me and to him I must have looked like a horny angel.

Having shared custard and made a few new friends we took an amble around the village taking in the non-cake related shops and the views, we strolled to the local church and I watched Michaela happily taking photographs of the ornate tombstones and gothic exterior of the church. Full of cake and coffee I was for the first time in a long time absolutely relaxed and blissfully happy.

I reflected on our time in the Peak District, I thought about the childhood memories Llangollen had stirred up and how now I was starting to look to the future. It started to feel less like I was running away from home and more like I was on holiday. I wondered to myself at what point do you cease to be running away from home and at what point have you run away from home and completed the task. Do you have to continuously have to keep moving or can you settle somewhere, if so for how long? At what point have you simply moved. Smiling at the questions Michaela found me mid grin. We sat a short while on the church bench with the silence and the sun.

Presently we was disturbed by the cackle of an obese pigeon on a quest for cake (he looked like he didn't mind boxed if you had it) we wandered back to the town to find the car, feeling suitably thirsty we decided a detour to the riverside pub was in order as a glass of wine and a non-alcoholic lager was in order.

Chapter Twenty-five: The Toole for the job

The Holy Island of Lindisfarne sits out on the North East coast of Northumberland, inherently beautiful; Holy Island has in many ways resisted the changing fashions of architecture and design. We drove over the causeway (eventually) after a few failed attempts my sense of timing and lack of ability to read the hydrographic website had conspired to have the tide work against us making any such endeavour peevishly fruitless. The Isle is just three miles by one and a half; it boasts a post office, a pub and a hotel. The residents take trips to mainland using Berwick upon Tweed for their groceries and other vestibules of modern life. There are no medical or professional services available on the island, it is a simple place and is perfect for any dreamer, poet or thinker.

Cut off for much of the day this tiny tidal Island has been a haven to many seeking peace and solitude for many centuries. First the Monks settled here cutting themselves off from the madness of the sixth century world, living simply from the land they brewed the best mead, created to fortify the body that god himself had created. I instantly liked the place, as two crows attempted murder in the hedgerow, we made our way through the small village streets to the ruined priory of Lindisfarne.

 As we walked through the once proud arches of the priory worn by the passing of time and the footsteps of the monks as they attended prayers six times a day, the views to the craggy beach and the coast beyond spun out below provocatively catching the eye and the soul, we made our way down through the old grounds the rocks and gravel crunched pleasingly against the bottom of our shoes, we headed towards the fruit gardens that reached out into the orchards beyond soon arriving on the sand. The north wind blew hard making its presence felt, even though our summer jackets it sent a stark chill to our bones each time it rose and fell. It seemed like a hard sort of place, once the summer and its visitors had gone it would undoubtedly have the capacity to give the local residents a hard time, and I drew my coat near me and surveyed the land.

I was taken back to a time, when I was young and working in London. No two places could be more different, in the serenity of Holy Island I was transported back by the call of a humble Seagull to the madness of a twentieth century Elephant and castle and a great time in my life. I remembered the Seagulls that had drifted down to the castle like a gang of bikers invading Brighton in Quadrophenia, were a far fresher bunch than the nervous and gentle beings circling my head as they called for scraps of anything going. The ones in London would have simply mugged me in a coordinated attack of shit and guns the lack of opposable thumbs being the only reason I suspect that I survived my tenure there.

Mum had moved away with her new partner to the Isle of Wight, My sister Cheryl and I had remained in London to seek out our own path in life, I was working at the time for a major clothing retailer, designated to assist in the running of their many branches. After some time working across Kent, Surrey and Essex as my experience grew, I could no longer fight off the inevitable transfer across to the dreaded London office. When London called you answered! Normally when you are in in retail it's with a resounding fuck off London.

Soon I landed in the Elephant and Castle or (stick it up your arsehole) branch as it was affectionately known by its victims. The travel from Kent was long and the workdays even longer, it was to say the least a tough gig. I was stationed in an old shopping centre much in need of a personality and an update. Long gone was its glory days, the day it first opened I imagined the Lord Mayor after cutting the ribbon being ushered to the nearest stairwell by centre management for a ceremonial piss in the stair well, after a quick shake and a zip up his good lady wife along with the rest of the ceremonial party was then ushered to the privacy of the lift where she too pissed offering her blessing while the erstwhile mayor declared the centre well and truly open for everyone's convenience (if not enjoyment), a tradition kept to this day by the local community.

Feeling alien to the community of Elephant and Castle, I was soon befriended by a fellow alien, Andy O' Toole. Andy from North London was around the same age and held many of the same interests. We found we had a mutual love of Playstation games, women, David Bowie and film, although our interests didn't necessarily follow that order. Andy arrived at the arsehole several months before me and knew which eateries had the potential to kill you and which shop owners would kill you given the chance. We bonded quickly and soon became good friends.

Slightly younger than me, a point he hastens to point out to me at any opportunity, he stood almost six foot, was well groomed and well kept, a bit of a contrast to myself, I always struggled and still do with clothes. Andy born all in proportion with his legs being the right length for his body made clothes look good, I on the other hand could be equally well dressed but alas I still always looked like I had just rocked in from a skip after a night in the police cell having received a right good drubbing from the Met's finest. He was earthy, friendly and always carried a smile.

Andy was the last really good true friend that I made, as I got older I found that I acquired mates and acquaintances rather than true and loyal friends, my grandad once said to me that you will get to an age where you will be able to count your friends on the fingers of one hand, at the time I thought that a stupid notion the bloody silly git, I remember wanting him just to move out of the way of the bloody telly so I could watch Bottom, but now I have reached a stage in life where I would give anything for his wisdom and experience.

More than twenty years after Andy and I first met I'm proud to say he still hasn't managed to get rid of me. We was bought up with similar backgrounds which was refreshing and unique as we both came from a council estates and we both were bought up solely by amazing mums on tight budgets, we understood the world we each inhabited and had much the same outlook. Growing up where I did was a blessing in many ways, but socially a lot of the friends I grew up with came from parents with professional backgrounds, although this never mattered to my friends sometimes though as I entered my teenage years it was hard to keep up with them, often I would have to excuse myself from weekend activities because a trip to the cinema or a day at a theme park would be a stretch too far for mum. I didn't mind but it separated me to some degree being slightly peripheral to the group.

Andy a proud North Londoner while I represented the South side understood my outlook and my values as I did his, we would find things external to work that we could both afford, there was no shame admitting I was skint as a lunch on the tab was always offered. We both now live many miles from London but when I think of London, I think of him and the start of my first career in retail.

Retail is a tough business to be in, the hours are long and your day was very much dictated by the attitude of the customers that you saw, you had the ones that knew their rights as they bought back the present aunt Aida had bought them three years previously that no longer fitted as it had been shrunk in a bizarre yet wholly true tumble drying incident. We had the ones that sniffed the change, the ones that sniffed themselves, the ones that attempted to sniff us and then you had the really strange ones.

One day Andy and I was messing around in the basement store room blissfully three floors away from the madness of the sales floor, we was listening to Bob Dylan while we found new and interesting ways to avoid the general public and the slightly hyperactive manager whose default setting was paranoid hysteria, he had the capability to move the needle only forward to panic and murder. I always thought he would explode as his red face would get redder and redder as the day wore on. Our reverie was soon interrupted as he burst through the stockroom doors red faced and in tears, squealing in a high pitched frenzy he declared that world war three had broken out in the store and everything was getting fucked up and that he wished he was dead.

Andy and I both recalled into our minds the current state of our finances, deciding a resignation or a walk out wasn't financially viable we left Bob singing about peace and justice as we ventured into world war three. Quickly assessing the situation a few things became alarmingly clear to me, I was the tallest and largest target on the war ground therefore the biggest prize and judging by the state of the trousers of the larger assailant it wasn't the mayor that had taken the ceremonial piss in a handbag.

It appeared that one of two geniuses was mid-way through smashing up the accessories stand as his wing man was spinning a bright red, slightly slutty handbag (which didn't suit him one bit) full of piss around knocking all the other handbags to floor while marinating everything else in piddle, I assumed that no one would have such a bright yet toothless smile on their face whilst being covered in someone else's piss from a slutty handbag (we was too far from Soho for all that). We had our culprit, if not the desire to apprehend him and now faced with the dilemma of getting covered in shit by the management or piss by the genius we really had a Hobson's choice. It was like a team of extras from deliverance had come out for a bit of practice. In the background I thought I heard a pig squeal, alas though it was just Steve the manager on the phone tendering his resignation between mouthfuls of pills.

Andy proved himself to be a handy and able human shield, after a few minutes of "want some do you, come on then, come on then" and "as long as I know where I stand mate" the police alighted their urban assault vehicle sending Tweedle Dum and Tweedle Stupid scattering down the high street like a pair of crack addicts running from their dealer, The police officers were slightly less motivated after what seemed like giving them to the count of twenty for a head start they ambled down the street behind them once they were sure that they had well and truly cleared the area, avoiding any complicated paperwork. The crisis was averted if only the same could be said for the handbag of piss and the matter of where we could borrow a mop, we was just finishing clearing up the mess when Steve's mum arrived taking him away in the back of her mini metro, never to be seen again.

Our early years and experiences like these had formed us, working in a tough borough had bonded us and as we got older, things like they often do change but the one thing that always remains is our ability to laugh at each other and with each other. The years for both of us have been hard at times. For Andy he has had many challenges on his journey, now a hugely successful software developer and an incredible and talented artist he is what I aspire to. His presence in my life makes me want to do better and be better.

Andy is a unique man, highly principled and complex he stands for what is right. His beliefs are his truth, he is one of the most honest and caring human beings I have the pleasure to have in my life. Never a prude or judgemental he walks his own path; he listens to advice willingly and questions the world with a natural intellectual curiosity of his own. I can go for ages without speaking to him but when we do eventually catch up together, we talk and laugh for hours on end as if no time had passed at all. He would give me his last pound and get covered in piss for me. Forever my human shield.

I smiled as Michaela and I sat in the priory café drinking a terrible coffee as I recalled my adventures in retail, Michaela asked me what had made me think of Andy while stood on the beach. I couldn't honestly think why myself; I had been rocked by laughter as far out among the rocks there was a couple hidden away from the world indulging in a little ladies and gentlemen, now never one to judge I had left them to their flagrante. Enthusiastically they were documenting their love via their camera phones. Deciding it was a moment best not shared I left them to it somewhat disturbed by the thought that such images conjured Andy to mind.

On the motorway south headed towards Lincoln a vision filled my head and the case of flagrante bringing about memories of Andy was solved, once while in China Andy had been required to take a photograph of his passport, while in the bath in his hotel he had the alert come through from the airline demanding that he send the photograph urgently to ensure a smooth check in, ever helpful Andy all alone in his hotel went in a state of undress to his drawers, placed his passport on the counter and took the photo, unfortunately in his haste he also sent Air France a picture of his dick, luckily for everyone involved as he assures me it was massive and the bath wasn't at all cold.

I have known Andy for many years, he has never been the most graceful person, but I always imagine the look he must have got from the poor soul on the check in desk. Mystery now solved and worryingly, so I realised that subconsciously I relate all naked people to Andy, I spent the entire journey in and out of giggles. The sacred and beautiful Holy Island, a place of peace and worship will forever in my mind conjure images of todgers.

As the grieving process played out within me, it became apparent that no one had given me the running order, pieces kept turning up unexpectedly, like characters in a play that you thought were dead. Parts that I thought I thought I was done with would pop back like an unwelcome uncle or a nagging aunt. The distance from home was gradually pulling me back to it; facing up to what had happened was inevitable and entirely unavoidable. The journey South I knew was going to be tough.

Sights and sounds would again become familiar, places and people that I knew would pass back into reality and the direction home was frightening, almost like a knowing acceptance that I was going back to my real life, back to normal and that all the things that made up the reality of my life would have to be slotted back in, I would have to face trials and tribulations without mum in my corner, I would have to do adulting all by myself. This feeling can be almost overwhelming.

Life as I knew it was bound to be different, I had no idea until I consciously thought about it as to just how many ways things would be different from the grand Christmas festivities to family holidays spent in complete bliss on the Isle of Wight with everyone. Like when you are trying to write a shopping list all the mundane things that you need allude your mind and pop up in the wrong order or in the wrong place, you then wander around the supermarket worrying that something vital had been forgotten which makes you angry with yourself.

Things change, the hardest part of death, apart from the obvious sense of loss is the change it brings and as human we are naturally predisposed to be avoidant of change but through the process of making small adjustments a different set of unique challenges opened up to present themselves to me like an old army major or a jaded sergeant in an old film.

Unsure that I was ready to face real life, I doubted that I was cut out to play the part of the anti-hero that goes up against the world worn sergeant in a series of scrapes that although funny teach him life lessons as the animosity between the two gives way to mutual respect, leading ultimately to acceptance and friendship, without mum nothing seemed possible, the chance of me successfully running my next bath or organising a drink in a brewery seemed like a distant prospect. When my mum died, my confidence went with her; everything you hold dear and believe in is questioned, not in a productive life changing way but in a way that takes your legs away from underneath you. I was going through hell and when you are going through hell, I thought the only thing you can do is keep going. Hell, on Holy Island I thought.

The best I could do for now was to accept the challenges in turn while I remained in the here and now, focusing on the new experiences and places I was yet to explore. As I stood on the holy island, I didn't find God, I found something better, I found the determination to carry on, to live, to experience and try and understand this beautiful planet that we merely hold a lease to. Stood with images of my friend's nut sack burned deep into my poor unfortunate mind I was resolute. I would never think of his balls again and I would try harder to understand the world better and seek knowledge that had so far eluded me, acceptance wasn't mine yet, but I understood it could be.

Chapter Twenty-six: Magna Carta, did she die in Vain?

Lincoln Cathedral is an extraordinary place, it is overwhelming in its size, home of the Magna Carta it is impressive, the trek towards the cathedral from the edge of the city was long and tiring, the cobbled streets twisted my ankles and the ever increasing gradient of the hill had me arriving at the coffee shop short of breath and in dire need of a cold drink. After best part of ten pounds was extracted from me, I concluded that the tourist trade in Lincoln must be flourishing and the prices were indeed at the level they are in the most tourist saturated parts of London.

This particular low lighted, led windowed brass filled horror had all the ambience of the plague, just without as much of the charm but a few more smells, the proprietor, a Mr Bastard I assumed was doling out meagre teaspoons of ice cream while attempting a world record to produce the world's most transparent glass of cola. If John Cleese had met this lot he would have had enough extra material for a third series of Fawlty Towers, Mr Bastard and his farty owls were in need of personality assessments and a quick go of being dragged around the town on a cross, tourists and school children could then be invited to pelt them with rotten fruit and small dollops of ice cream, this I felt was very much in keeping with the lineage of the City.

After a genuine, yet inadvertently free Lincoln prison experience delivered by the wonderful Mr bastard we pressed on spotting a policeman I stopped to ask him how much further we had to go to reach the Cathedral, I was cress fallen to learn that we had made it just under halfway up the hill where the Cathedral sat, I gathered then that given the height God himself must live in there. I wondered what the penalty would be for stealing a mobility scooter but soon the idea passed as I doubted even the best ones available on the market would be able to handle the now insanely steep gradient. As the hill steepened and the closer you got to the Cathedral the parking prices increased, another arsehole town clerk with a plan, Lincoln had things all sewn up.

The trek up the hill was worth it, the cathedral gleamed in the brilliant late august sun, horses with carriages arrived and departed with happy smiling visitors. Families took selfies as coach groups by the hundred arrived swarming like intoxicated bees hurrying to the entrance before one of them died. Asthmatics in the recovery position littered the pavement as larger members of the various groups joined them in their attempts to get air back into their lungs.

The effort was worth it, a short distance from the cathedral is Lincoln Castle, a well preserved medieval castle boasting within its grounds a Victorian prison and unique chapel, The castle has to be one of the best preserved and unmolested in the county, the home of the original magna carta since 1215 it is one of only two castles in the united Kingdom to boast two Mottes, the other being Lewes in East Sussex. William Marwood the infamous nineteenth century hangman and champion of the long drop hanging method, preferring to break the necks of his clients rather than have them suffocate to death (for this I still don't think we can give him any credit as a nice human being).

After a walk around the parapets and through the old ancient roman thoroughfares we arrived at the room that held the Magna Carta a self-imposed hush seemed to fall over us, the very existence of such a precious document made me feel proud to be British, our respect for law and order and our reverie for our history filled me with joy. Here I was with something that had seen every single one of our prime ministers come and go, this beautifully written and brilliantly coloured document, our guarantee of freedom and our right to live without oppression had seen off two world wars and now to me it seemed to be the most important thing in the world. The least I could have done to see it was to put up with drinking the world's crapiest cola and climb the world's steepest hill.

A short walk and almost fifty pounds later we were stood in the coolness of the cathedral, its interior was welcome, it was much brighter than I expected its columns and archways pushing up to the sky as if they could go on forever. Not being religious myself I was conscious not to disturb the many people there who fell silent in prayer, in a way I envied those with faith as I hoped for them death had a happy ever after. It was something that their faith could help them make sense of. I smiled at the wide variety of people sat quietly praying, thinking, wishing and hoping. The usual suspects, the textbook antiques roadshow viewers were joined by the young and people from all walks of life, society seemed to be held in a microcosm, I liked it. My favourite was a Vyvyan from the young ones look alike sat in the back with his eyes closed deep in thought, alongside him sat what looked like Cyndi Lauper, it was reassuring and beautiful to see.

I was surprised that my Uncle Brian had faith towards the end of his life; he was larger than life in many ways, funny, intelligent and very well-travelled he was the ultimate man of the trees, he loved nature and was a tree surgeon by trade, I spent one summer working with him when I was fifteen he taught me about the soil and to love what you do, there is no point otherwise he boomed. I miss him terribly, I really didn't know him too well as life often got in the way, not caring about relationships time so often turns us into strangers, in later life we became close and just as I was getting to know him as an adult he was taken from us way too young and full of life, My uncle Paul and I would meet Brian once a week and visit pubs and places from Brian's youth. We would sit chatting away for hours on end long into the night, I had finally crafted a proper adult relationship with them both when Brian suffered a massive heart attack in his back garden at home a few days after

Paul and I last saw him, he died instantly. It was my first experience with death as an adult and it was painful. I smile now when I think of him because I knew him well.

I was honoured but heartbroken when I gave his eulogy at his funeral; this great gentle and wonderful man was taken away from us and it was unfair, I have his little sapling knife to this day. It sits in my office desk drawer with a small bottle of my mum's perfume. I have in my display case a small wade Tom figurine, from Tom and Jerry that Brian bought for my mum for her birthday in 1973, it connects them both to me and I love it. When I went to pick it up from my sister Donna's house, she had written a little note on it, "it's time this cat went back home".

Paul has been my constant throughout my life, a father figure to me, always in my corner he is one of the coolest people I know. He reminds me so much of my mum, his temperament, kindness and even temper is uncanny. In the early years he had the coolest cars arriving to our house in his trademark yellow Ford Capri his long hair being the ultimate accessory to his styled Rod Stewart look. Paul always made sure we were Ok, helping mum out at times when she needed it, he perfectly played the part of the unassuming hero.

As I moved into my teens, he was there for me, buying me my first of many illegal pints, leaving my mum to buy my first legal one on my eighteenth birthday. When mum moved away to the Isle of Wight, I was seventeen. He kept an eye on me making sure we was always fed and watered he made sure that we was OK, Life hasn't always been easy like everyone he has had his challenges, he has the unique ability to rise to meet them dispensing his own brand of humour, wisdom and knowledge. Paul always brings an altruistic intelligence to any situation; he doesn't get to wear a cape but to me he is very much a hero. He is my hero and I love him dearly.

I was shaken from my thoughts as Michaela grasped my hand, keen to get back out into the sunshine we walked up the centre of the aisle towards the doors, I took one last look behind me as the sun flooded my eyes and the splendid heat of the august afternoon took our breath away. We walked around the cathedral appreciating the sheer size and magnitude of its exterior. In stark contrast to this beautiful fissure we were headed to our hotel on the South to Lincolnshire coast, Skegness was our destination. I was looking forward to spending some time there after Sue Townsend had written so brilliantly about it in her Adrian Mole books.

Chapter Twenty-seven: Give the man your right bollock Bert

Bert Baxter would have given his right Bollock for a week away in Skegness, Pandora however was somewhat unconvinced. Adrian Mole, the anti-hero from the brilliant mind of the Wonderful Sue Townsend has been one of my favourites for many years, the tragic loss of his creator at such a young age left us in his last book on a cliff hanger, we know that the car belonged to Pandora, Adrian's unrequited love of his life having arrived at his house Adrian and Pandora walk towards each other where the book ends, we will now never know how that story played out. A real Schrodinger of a problem. We are now left with two truths in the first Adrian and Pandora walk towards each other as Pandora realises her only love has ever been the humble Adrian Mole and they live happily ever after, the second and equally possible prospect is Pandora tells Adrian to stop dreaming and move on. Each one both true in our minds as the answer sadly will never come.

In the television adaptations starring the brilliant Julie Walters, the late Stephen Moore and Gian Sommarco in the protagonist's role. Skegness held a special place for me, we had been fleetingly in Blackpool a few days previously and we couldn't help but draw upon the similarity of the two. I wanted to retrace the steps that Moley took and see if I could still some of the landmarks. I was pleased to be spending a few days here. The weather was warm, and the funfair rides were singing accompanied by whistles and screams. The whole place was alive. The proletariat were out in force, we joined them.

The world can be a totally crackers place, Skegness is a microcosm of the universe that has lost the plot. It has all sorts of strange about it with something for everyone included along with added salt and sugar, sometimes I wish the world was more like Skegness offering something for everyone, bathed in sunshine accompanied by acoustic laughter track. I'm saddened that often the world isn't that way for the many, but here in Skegness we witnessed the garish green lights and out of season tinsel by the yard, probably hung just in time for Sid James and Barbara Winsor to do the honours of turning on the lights for the 1972 season. As we walked, we was serenaded by the waling of sirens and the clatter of coin boxes of the penny arcade machines offering everything in prizes from a dry hump and durex through to I-phones and then there was the star prize, the elixir of eternal youth itself, machines filled with coins by the desperate, pissed and the needy. Stacks of ten pence pieces were greedily consumed as world worn fey attendants quietly told happy guests to go fuck themselves under their breath.

If you take a short diversion in any direction you land on the quiet beach or a green, the sounds of the waves crash against the cheerful organ music in a chorus of faded grandeur. Skegness is a town that is quite unique as it appears to be completely arsehole and poser free, the visitors and residents seem to have looked up from their Twitter and media accounts and realised that there is a real world out there and they treat it as a real place, although some people seem to be witnessing it with a temporary facelift provided by lashings of potato and hop derived alcohol but they don't document every living moment by way of a selfie. It was barmy and brilliant; it was everything that a town like Hastings used to be. Skegness is a place that will have a cheeky look up your skirt and will playfully nudge you in the ribs, it may even run off with your wife it has that spirit of enjoyment about it. I was surprised by just how much I liked it. Even the local vagrants seemed to be enjoying the sunshine accompanied by premium brand methylated spirits, in Hastings things are different, the only treat is a quick stab up an alley and no kiss on lips, other than the odd bank holiday it is as soulless as it is joyless.

Skegness reminded me a lot of Margate when it and I were in our heyday, sadly when Michaela and I had travelled back there while in Kent the place was on its knees like a battered old aunt with soppy hands. The Dreamland theme park had long closed and was a derelict waste ground it was a sad place, The shutters were down across the old sea front shops they were beautifully decorated with the obligatory pictures of cocks and tits in varying sizes and colours, the beach itself remained almost empty and the locals looked pretty vacant too, I looked at a postcard in one of the few remaining shops and I was transported back to my childhood by scenes of people eagerly queuing to enter the dreamland theme park created by the legendary Bem Bom brothers. Many a happy hour me and the gang spent at Dreamland in the early eighties, we would go, like Del boy and the jolly boys on a coach with the local social club with the kind volunteers that gave up their time to take us each summer, Lee, Daniel and I always went with a revolving rota of friends interchanging on each visit. The grand sum of four pounds plus a bit for the arcade and some lunch would cover us, I have always been drawn to the sea and the coast and for me it was the best thing ever.

I was told by a friend a story that not long after the new Tate gallery was opened on the front they had a visiting artist whose art involved him sitting nicely funded by the lottery counting to one million (I'd prefer geese in flight myself) on the day he was due to reach the milestone of a million the press and some locals (perhaps disappointed that there wasn't one spray painted cock or tit to be seen) had gathered to witness the event, as the artist arrived at the one million mark and the press were poised to celebrate the stupidity of the whole thing a voice from the crowd shouted "coming ready or not!". The very thought of this reminded me of my uncle Brian who would have revelled in this story.

Brian set out forty years ago to travel India, in the summer of 1980 he and his girlfriend Myra (despite what life dealt them, I still believe even now that Myra was always his person) set off for parts unknown, travelling through India and through the pacific basin he lost himself in the world, exchanging pensions and savings for experience and adventures, something that I'm so glad he managed to do, he didn't live long enough to need either, but he lived. He never chased a dream because he didn't need to. He chose life and lived it his way. His diary from his travels all those years ago was found after he died.

The diary sat for many years unread but in the fullness of time Paul had it typed up so it could be read, as I read his diary all those years later in fact almost a decade after he died each word painted in my mind echoed of his voice and for an all too brief moment Brian was back in the room with me for one last adventure. Foolishly now when I miss Brian (which to my surprise is often) I don't think of him as dead, I tell myself he is travelling across India again and he is at peace, to be honest I think more and more that in death anything was possible especially in the fantastically wonderful life of Brian. You can become part of place, or leave your mark upon it as much as it does on you, Peter Kay is as synonymous with Blackpool as the Beatles and Cilla Black are to Liverpool, a person can become part of place by association or merely by a memory. Brian is in my mind synonymous with my silly place, where laughter is compulsory, and the spirit of adventure and childhood remain forever young.

The magic is all around in Skegness you just have to know where to look and today I looked at it through Brian's eyes, it's only when you leave the place that you appreciate it, like the Scotsman that hasn't lived in Scotland for fifty years he still misses it. I'm yet to hear a song about Scotland that doesn't involve missing it in same way or lamenting to return, Billy Connolly summed it up best when he said "once the song is finished the reality is there is no fucking way the singer has any intention of returning back, the fact they found the bus out in the first place was a miracle". I don't think many songs have been sung about Skegness but the people I met and spoke to there were all having a great day and were all at varying levels of pissed the alcohol consumption outstripping that of sugar which by any standard was impressive. As the day wore on Michaela and I settled on the beach with an impromptu picnic procured from the local Morrisons, as we sat dining on the finest scotch eggs and pork pies two dogs made sweet love for our entertainment and enjoyment as the waves rolled in.

When you talk to people enjoying a day out or on holiday I always detect that there is always a sort an eagerness for them to explain their life decisions to you, like the Harry Enfield character that feels compelled to apologise to everyone he speaks to about the war everyone was friendly and had a story, we heard from Eadie from Dunbartonshire who was recovering nicely from a suppurating ulcer on her leg, Sheila from Daventry that was sick of her husband knocking her about and finally a pissed up Meg who decried that she" loves that man I do, fucking love him, the nasty bastard" the one thing that they all had in common was compulsion to explain to us that Skegness is the Blackpool of the East, how poetic I thought. As we finished our food and we open heartedly applauded the floor show as a dog who we now knew was called Monty was now being berated and playfully beaten, to be fair he seemed unrepentant, shagged-out and pretty happy about the whole affair.

His co-conspirator had since been spirited away no doubt to a farm in the country to enter into a period of rehabilitation and behavioural correction "your massive slut dog Gifty! you whore!" no doubt would ring out far and wide. I laughed at the amount of effort and anxiety being expelled over a quickie between a Greyhound and a Cockerpoo. As we walked the promenade our eyes were drawn to the old and now long defunct railway company adverts that adorned the walkway advertising Skegness as the Blackpool of the East, a kindly fisherman peered back at us from the retro print declaring Skegness to be bracing as he skipped merrily along the sand. Realizing that I was slowly being indoctrinated into the cult of Skegness being the Blackpool of the east, I feared that some sort of inferiority complex was washing over the place, I wanted to shout " it's not bloody Blackpool get over it", dappy bastards this place was much better and far less cynical.

The day light started to fade as we walked along the sand swept road to the Skegness pier which was opened in 1881 by the civil engineering firm Clarke and Pickwell it was once the fourth largest pier in the country, in 1978 the pier was badly damaged by a severe storm which led ultimately to demolition of some of the original features, by the mid-1980s the pier had significantly changed from its original T-shaped form to be the straight affair it is now. As I neared the end of the pier the relatively newly appointed railings greeted me, to my joy along the railings was hundreds of padlocks, locked tightly to the weather-beaten railings each padlock had the names or initials of couples etched or written on them, I loved that a faceless bureaucrat hadn't ordered there removal and destruction, they had made them part of the place, a place for lovers and love to behold. After firmly attaching my newly purchased padlock to the railing GM and MB took their place in Skegness history and became a part of the community, Uncle Brian on slight detour smiled on.

We had managed to navigate our way around the country using all sorts of Hotels, Bed and breakfasts and sometimes even a quiet layby when neither was available. We had stayed in some expensive places and some not so. The cost of a hotel room per night didn't seem to reflect the friendliness of the staff that kept them going some of our cheapest stays had been amongst the most friendly and comfortable, I admit I'm not one for servants or savants and the prospect of fawning bell hops and butlers leave me cold. The hotel in Skegness left me nothing to fear on those fronts as after travelling through every county in the UK we managed to find the country's worst hotel, Basil Fawlty would have registered a complaint and his parrot having stayed here would most certainly be grateful that it was dead.

Upon entering Guest house bastard (not it's real name to protect the innocent) was just off the sea front and was an obvious Mecca for seagull's and a designated potty for their effluvium at first I thought these great white menaces of the sky were squealing at us deriding our hotel choices but as we entered it was soon apparent that the gulls were in fact laughing at us. A hotel that advertised that it offered lights and tea in every room was always going to be exciting and we were about to find out just how so.

The Lobby was so run down and rough even the arms of the chairs had tattoos on them, the owner surprised at having a guest removed his pen from behind his ear and his finger from his nose filled out some paperwork on what I am sure was merely a post it note, after ensuring we wasn't "poofters or degenerates" he presented us from a tin behind his desk two sad little tea bags, un wrapped and crumpled, almost smiling he past us two small milk pouches as he explained that if he continued to put such treasures in the rooms he would be bankrupt, Onslow here had a morbid obsession that guests would as soon as they checked in be passing tea, coffee, sugar and all other manner of consumables out the windows to their friends as all guests were either "poofs, degenerates, ropey looking men in dresses or robbing bastards". Things went downhill from there.

As Onslow waited for death to release him (he must have built up a resistance over many years as his fascinating skin diseases and botulism had yet to claim him) he watched us walk towards the stairs to our room, "don't use the handrail" he called it isn't attached, stifling a laugh I assured him to his relief that we didn't expect any form of safety features and that making it through the night alive was merely an added bonus to our a stay not a requirement he cheered up cracking a toothless smile as he invited us to fuck off and die in our rooms while enjoying the complimentary lighting while eating him out of house and home.

Our room was to say the least basic, the lighting so frivolously boasted in the brochures was on the blink, the bed was some sort of door nailed to a bed frame. The mattress I assumed was famed in history as one used in the 1983 bed wetting world championships where it had sustained ten gallons of aqua vita from Mrs Aida Perkins the Runcorn and district regional champion, the stains loving preserved for the future enjoyment of mankind. The bathroom tiles were so sticky they lifted up with each step you took and pulled years of slime from the floor with them, the bathroom suite was grey with age and dirt, the shower curtain was blackened at the hem with spots of mould, realising there was in fact no shower to compliment the curtain made me chuckle, it was that or the fumes from the spores of mould that gathered on the rotting window frames that were enthusiastically infusing my lungs.

After a short drive to the supermarket to get a some cleaning materials and two sleeping bags we agreed our survival strategy, we agreed that we would wash the bathroom down and use the cardboard boxes we had gathered from our shopping trip to lay on the bathroom floor when it was cleaned, one of us would sleep in the cleaned bath with the curtain pegged up on its sad little wire and the other on the boxes, we would then at the crack of dawn make our escape and head to Suffolk and the mighty Landguard fort. At 430am our plan was completed, stifling a laugh we retreated, we had a fort to conquer.

Chapter Twenty-eight: Goodies and Baddies

After our daring escape from the hotel we were pleased to be alive, the night had passed by with very little sleep, but with the spirit of London during wartime flowing through our veins we got through it, just before the sun was in the sky we crept down the stairs remembering not to use the hand rail and to my delight Onslow was asleep on a little camp bed behind his little desk, I knew then that I would remember him for the rest of my life, he was one of those people that will eventually die out as the world sleepwalks towards online reviews and feedback these places will wither away, as I drove towards the county lines I couldn't help but wonder if that was a good thing or not, after all a bastard is a bastard whether he is in a dress or not.

We arrived in Felixstowe a little before seven. Hungry we found a small café getting ready for another day's trade, the owner a friendly looking man was heaving bottles of milk into his small but welcoming establishment. The smell of warm grease and coffee hung pregnant in the air. We enjoyed what was a fine breakfast, I over did it on the bacon as usual and with full stomachs we watched the boats drifting in and out of the harbour, the morning sun had grown steady in the sky and was now splendid above the water the ripples sparkled and they eased their way to the shore. We watched the town come to life as people started about their normal business, buses shuttled the workers to the docks for another day of graft. The streetlights hummed as they shut down for another late summer day.

Landguard fort is one of the finest of its type built as a basic earthwork structure in 1540 it was soon updated and extended by James 1st of England, coming to real prominence in 1717 it was greatly extended and by 1780 it had taken the shape that it is today, the only relatively modern addition is the world war two influenced Darell's Battery where operation Outward was masterminded, when thousands of balloons were launched from the site festooned with explosives bound for Germany whereby upon contact with power lines would cause them to explode interrupting precious electricity resources for the Germans.

This stroke of genius was like many things created from accident, in 1940 a storm blew across the flats of Suffolk and 6 barrage balloons were broken loose from their moorings, reports were soon received from as far away as Sweden and Denmark, some reaching as far as Finland. The reports of the damage created when the balloons landed the damage was great and disruption to allied forces affected was huge, this gave the British war office an idea and Operation Outward was born. By the end of the program almost one hundred thousand balloons had been launched causing mayhem to enemy forces.

Operation Outward was extended to other key facilities across the UK, the most successful launch was from Oldstairs Bay near Dover where a balloon launched hit a high voltage cable at Leipzig causing a malfunction at the Bohlen powerplant burning it to the ground. The estimated damage according to German records accessed in 1946 was in excess of fifty-five million pounds although the figure is understood to be much higher due to the incomplete nature of wartime information that wasn't known to always be accurate.

We made our way along the coast arriving at Landguard fort as it opened, my eye as always was drawn to the Darell's Battery, two imposing concreate towers stared back at me as resolute as the day they were completed, I thought back to all the childhood games we used to play as kids, sticks would become makeshift machine guns as tales of daring bravery played out in our minds, a type of storytelling mapped out as we wove plots and twists into our games. Like the plots from Clint Eastwood movies tell us there are always the good guys and the bad guys and whoever was late to our game (for whatever the reason, no excuses) invariably would be allowed to join the game as a baddy taking their chances of receiving a good kick in the nuts for being Rommel, a blow to the head was the least you could expect.

As Childhood games gave way to teenage angst goodies and baddies ruled the playground, at secondary school, things were far more complex. It was challenging time for me, I had liked junior school and had settled well with many friends and of course my beloved gang, I had great friends outside of school and my days were filled with fun and laughter. I struggled at first to integrate into Secondary school, A few faces from Tubbenden had followed me to Secondary School but none that were really my friends, the gang was gone, and things were hard. I found it difficult to find a way through the day, I eventually began to hate school. The carefree days messing about with Ben, Danny and the school gang were over.

Things were made worse at school by my lack of enthusiasm for football which seemed to be almost a requisite for acceptance, my hatred for PE, Maths and French was only bested by my dislike of the teachers. I have known mostly excellent teachers in my life, both as a student and as their friends (just don't mention the holidays and the hours and you will get along fine!). I soon found that the only escape channel I had was through English, History and Drama classes, they became anchor points in my day as I navigated bullying teachers and peers alike. Here I was again playing a game of war with the good guys and the bad guys.

One afternoon as I dashed towards one of the interhouse school Drama events, I was intent on keeping my head down and avoiding eye contact for fear of coming into contact with any of my tormentors in the busy hallways. I hated this place with a passion and soon I was sure that I would become a statistic, I was soon caught up by one of the lads in my form, a hansom lad that was popular around school with the sports fanatics and more importantly with the girls, "you going to drama?" he chimed, I nodded in response and set about on my way feeling almost relieved as I arrived to the safety of the Drama theatre. I wasn't aware then that this interaction was the first I was to have with one of most favourite people on the planet, My lifelong friend Justin Holmes, the kindest and sweetest guy I have had the pleasure to have known, in any Clint Eastwood or in Justin's case Arnie film he would have been the leading goodie.

At the start of each production we would complete voice and breathing exercises led by perhaps my favourite teacher of all time Mrs House, a teacher with energy and passion not only for her subject but for us children. She cared passionately about life, art, and people. As we finished chanting our key words and had limbered up Justin again came to say Hi, we soon started talking and as is his natural charm and kindness we were soon friends, things are always better when Justin is around, they are more fun, impish and above all calm. His greeting "hello sailor!" was soon the highlight of my day and the dark thoughts and mood I was experiencing soon lifted. I don't think to this day Justin understands how he pulled me from the parapet of self-destruction.

It was through Justin that I met my good friend Chris and soon two other lads Matthew and Terry completed our group, we enjoyed each other's company and found our place, the bullying for me unfortunately lasted throughout my entire secondary education but with my group of friends it was fleeting and I coped. By my fourth year at school I was in my stride and I only really had issues with a few of the lads, kids can be horrible. I choose not to judge them in retrospect, I hope that they grew into good and kind people who reject that type of behaviour. The damage that can be done with a few unkind words can be so hurtful, perhaps more so than we imagine.

The memories of those golden times edged between the moments of terror at secondary school combined by the sure walls of the fort made me feel grown up, as if I had moved past the point of caring about people from my past that added no value.

Each year there would be a school drama production, this looking back was the best time of my life, I made a small group of friends collected from my time on the production and I remembered a while ago when I was going through some old boxes at home and I discovered an old VHS tape of the play and to my delight crammed on at the end was some behind the scenes footage of us all messing about before and after the play, our young faces, some that I had long forgotten looked back at me and for the first time I smiled about my secondary school tears, I couldn't remember the last time I had seen the grained and somewhat decayed footage and I felt even less sure why I hadn't had such a positive reaction to it before, in my mind I simply assumed that I wasn't ready then but now I understood that even in times of great provocation there is friendship, laughter and fun.

Now, here on the tip of the East coast I let a let a lot of my pent-up shit go, I let the negativity out and I sobbed. It was a cathartic feeling as a weight lifted from my shoulders. I was finally free of the past; I had just decided to let it all go. This spring cleaning of my mind I knew was needed in other aspects of my life, I was growing as a person, accepting hurt and loss while learning from it. Although my physical journey was coming to an end, I thought then that I had a lot more to deal with in my own mind, but I knew I was ready to make those changes and accepting them was the first stage.

Chapter Twenty-nine: Isle travel with you

This Island of ours is a wonderful place, we are a blessed nation. We are surrounded on all sides by seas and oceans with the most wonderful coastlines to compliment them; we can walk on a beach in the morning and be at the top of a mountain in the afternoon. We have a history pedigree that is envied the world over.

This little island is diverse, full in the most part with honest, hardworking and friendly people, some as curious as the buildings they inhabit. We are a proud nation of shop keepers, beekeepers, innovators and engineers. Our stamp on the world is a heritage to be proud of, from the garden of England to the angel of the north examples of human spirit runs through our blood.

We gave the world half of Laurel and hardy and all of Chaplin, our writers, poets and thinkers are revered the world over from Dickens to Shakespeare via Leslie Thomas and David Nobbs they have entertained the world through their craft. As Isambard Kingdom Brunel changed the way we travel, Bertrand Russell changed the way we think. Our contribution to the world can never be measured, as the Who and the Beatles rocked out with the Rolling Stones Galton and Simpson wrote scripts from the geniuses Tony Hancock and Harry H. Corbett.

Alec Guinness made us laugh in the Ealing comedy films such as kind hearts and coronets and the lady killers. The Carry-on Films with the wonderful Sid James, Kenneth Williams, Hattie Jacques and Joan Sims forever carry on willing us never to lose our head. We can even lay claim to the humble Bakewell Tart and the heated butter knife. Whatever way I looked at it I felt that I had all this history and innovation on my doorstep but sinfully I had never bothered to look, maybe that is a bit harsh I don't think it would have occurred to me look. Now, suitably chastised whenever I walk down the most suburban of streets, I look upwards, downwards and sideways. If you look hard enough you will the echoes of the past all around you. The Victorian plumbing, old wartime resistance markers as well as some of the most beautiful buildings in the world.

Perhaps I do like to brag but I'm very proud of what our forefathers and mothers did before us, and I feel a sense of Kinship with them. I feel the world is merely leased to us and we are its custodians. When I'm sat in a field surrounded by the hills and trees or by the water's edge or one of Eugenius Birch's piers, I can't help but feel blessed with it. I have a new and exciting relationship with the outdoors and nature, in a way I have mum to thank for that as it was my situation that led me to the outdoors and Michaela that fed my love for it. To my two favourite ladies I owe a debt of gratitude. I love you both completely and utterly, I always will.

As I reflected on our journey, it had taken us through every county in the country, across the waterways, through caves, over mountains and over many miles of roads, we had stayed In some fantastic hotels, some of them with real mini size bars of imperial leather soap in them which absolutely pissed with sophistication. Some even had a working television to which we would eagerly connect up our portable DVD as we fell tired in to bed each evening, we managed to miss the ending to the brilliant film stand by me eight times in as many nights before we gave it up too tired from the copious amounts of walking and eating we did.

I had driven the length of Hadrian's wall across the top of Scotland from coast to coast, walked through Sherwood forest and visited each tip of the four ridings of Yorkshire. Wales had been a splendid host. The Midlands surprised me the most as I travelled on boats deep underground through its caves and travelled its rails with my heart on my sleeve and my head rather naughtily out of the window. From Rutland water to Pembrokeshire I had run to them all, learning and searching for sanity and calm.

The months had caught up with me and I was tired, the balminess heat of summer was waning, children had disappeared from the parks and gardens to don their school uniforms and embark on a new school year full of promise and opportunity, far away in the distance if you timed it right you could hear the children at play, carefree and happy. Their school trips still ahead of them and the best friends that will ever know to the side of them. I envied them slightly as I closed my eyes, I drank in the ringing of children's laughter from the playground I swear that I heard a shrill voice I scream "remember it's my game!" I smiled contently as I let the last few months wash over me, I laid back my eyes still tightly shut I felt the cool grass gently welcome me. I don't know how long I had been laying there as my head filled with thoughts of friends, love and loss. Soon I knew I would be home. I was going home.

The four most precious words on anyone's lips must be "hi mum, I'm home". For those who are blessed to still say those words I would encourage you to do it loud and do it often. Travelling back from roads well-travelled to the familiar front door that used to be the gateway to your whole world and stepping inside without even a care of a knock is to me now a blissful memory as your senses are filled with the sights and smells of childhood that hypnotise you like a child watching Christmas lights dance in the darkness. Then the familiar call of your mum asking if you want a cup of tea as the kettle already engaged with split timing accuracy bubbles away to itself. The catch-up conversation as you both talk about your day and fill one another in on all the family gossip and as the last dregs of tea is drunk you fall back to your old childhood bedroom which stands as it was then. Soft fragrant smelling towels scent the room as you drift off to sleep without a care in the world. The safety of home breathes with you as you slumber.

After our many adventures together, I had one final stop that I wanted to make on my own before I headed home. I gathered myself together and was soon at the Cemetery, as I switched my phone off I noticed my hands were cold, the air was crisp and it nipped as it moved in waves of its own, the sound of the sea a short distance away gently washed into my ears and cleansed my consciousness. The summer was over and the autumnal sun though lingering was at odds with the earth, the flowers and trees swayed gently in unison with the easy breeze. The smell of fresh cut grass, balmy hazes and chirping of the skylarks was over, I was in a melancholy mood and as I walked, I surmised that even summer must pass although now in the moment the flowers and trees still protested.

Patio sets and barbecues would soon be packed away for the winter awaiting the sun to return sometime never, as lawns had their final cut of the year winter coats were surely set to be coming out of cupboards and the space filled with presents as we all try to get ahead of Christmas.

There are several things that over the last few months I had learnt about the universe and my place in the great order of things. The time we have to dance on this earth is painfully short, in the grand scheme of things our lives are as fleeting as a daydream you have while at work on an idol Wednesday afternoon.

Part of life is death, and all the hellos and handshakes make the goodbyes harder. I had spent such a long time existing in death's shadow, trying to quantify the pain of losing mum, trying to process all the anger and bite down on the rage at the fucking unfairness of it all. I realised that I had chosen pain. I had allowed the beast in; it dined at my table and lay at my feet. I had chosen it, not it me.

I had chosen simply to function, to silently get through and to exist the best I could with the bitter hand I had been dealt. Now I was angry but not with the world but with myself, I had missed the most important thing, the lesson that mum had taught me all along, I had missed it because I was too involved in grief and emotion to see it was staring me in the face, my realization was simple as long as you remember the ones you have lost, they are never gone, they live forever. After all if mum's life was a book would I still read it knowing that the end was going to be too tough to bare and I knew from that moment that everything was going to be OK I was going to be Ok, life would be good again and mum as always would push us onwards. The world, her world was such a beautiful place. It always had been.

Life is full of first and lasts, I realised the moments in between are the most important, Mum was with me when I open my eyes for the first time and took my first breath, she saw me take my first steps, say my first words and she mended countless skinned knees and broken hearts. She made it impossible for me to fail and gave me the confidence to believe I could do anything, even write a book if I wanted to, when she knew she was dying she gave me her blessing and encouragement to write our story, I was there when mum closed her eyes for the last time. I arrived at her bed, my sisters were there mum was gasping for breath fighting with every last drop of her resilience, Cheryl in her wisdom quietly whispered to mum that I had arrived as Donna held mums hand, mum looked up to check I was there, making sure we was all together, She was fighting for her life to make sure we was all together, the bravest and most incredible lady. Mum's bold piercing blue eyes looked into my soul and with no words I understood she was ready; it was time and without words she understood we was going to let her go. For a year I prayed to God or anyone would listen to keep her alive for my sake, now I sat silently praying that God would take mum for her sake. Mum stopped gasping and she became calm, in calm and silence of those chilly minutes of uncertainty Donna told mum to go be with her boy and we would all be okay. I had never been prouder of her she held mum's hand and spoke softly to her. Donna is an incredible woman and every bit as strong as mum, her gift to all of us.

The wind moved once again in from the sea and sound of seagulls woke me from my reverie, I strolled through the gates of the cemetery. Gravestones lay out like an ocean, a sea of poignant markers each one of a life lived, hellos and goodbyes by the thousands, the headstones stood in graceful silence echoing stories told and neatly filed away, some were weathered and beaten some cherished. All somebody's darling. Artefacts confirming, we lived, and we died. My favourite headstones are the funny ones. As I wondered through the many graveyards and cemeteries on my travels (the difference I learnt from a lady met in Bakewell, she told me in hushed tones befitting a graveyard that a Cemetery is only a cemetery when it is attached to a church, a graveyard is of course therefore sans a church) I saw my favourite inscription on headstone on Holy Island in Northumberland it read "I came to be without being consulted and I leave here without my consent". I loved the humour of the piece I loved how someone even in death gave the gift of laughter.

This though was not how my journey was going to end; I had now my absolute truth everything was going to be alright, different but alright. I knew soon I would leave this place as now I couldn't think of one reason why I felt it was important for me to come back here at all, I was certain then as I am now that I would never come back, mum wasn't here. She never was. She is all around me, when I look in the mirror to shave in the morning, she is looking back at me, she has gifted us her legacy only I was in too much in pain to see it. She is in my sisters and my sons, my nephews and nieces. She is the ability we have to be ourselves; she is the kindness we see in others. She is the warm breeze that lifts us when we are cold and every butterfly I see. She isn't a tombstone, under the earth; those markers are for someone else I have no use for them.

Her mark is that she was our greatest gift and our blessing; yes, selfishly I wish like everyone that met her that we could have had her for longer of course we do, but it wasn't to be. The longing that we have when one we love dies is the human in us all. I wish desperately for one last conversation and as I lay in bed some nights unable to sleep when rods of reason crash through my head as I search for answers that won't come, I wish for one more piece of advice, for one more helping hand or and now in this moment I would settle for one of her smiles.

Mum is gone, she isn't ever coming back that is the tough price of love and it is a debt that must always be paid. The price to have a beautiful star and an angel with the gentlest of souls as a mother is steep and we all in our own ways have paid dearly that debt.

 I have the serenity within me now to accept that however much I follow my star I won't find its end; this I know is the true. I won't find her until my own journey is at an end and we will meet and that for me is OK. In the meantime, and until that time comes, I take comfort that I take her wisdom forward with me, I have the echo of her laughter in my ears and her memory in my heart, for always.

Since losing mum I often think to myself that when my time comes mum will be there to meet me, waiting patiently on a bench surrounded by pleasant green fields, wild ducks and a babbling brook, I will get to call her Mumma again and to my abject joy she will answer, I can't imagine her voice anymore as I can't remember it. Maybe the absence of memory will make her response sound so much sweeter. Even now I can't watch home movies of her with the volume on.

Now, I was done with this place and as I walked a warm breeze blew in to shield me, I didn't look at the grave or the cemetery I didn't need to I smiled at the thought that Michaela was waiting for me and home although still a long way off was in my heart and part of me looked forward to the drive home and a much needed cheeky hamburger for dinner. In Michaela I had my person, my rock and my everything. I have a wonderful family gifted to me by my mum.

The journey was over, what I was looking for through all the many miles and through all the places I had been was with me and inside me all along. My redemption song was singing, it was time to go home. No longer a runaway but part of something.

My thoughts were with me all the way to the car and as I ambled slowly through the iron cemetery gates I switched my phone back on and it immediately started to ring, I answered, my life was about to change again forever………………